Late Diagnosed AuDHD

A Complete Guide for Adults Living Authentically with Autism and ADHD Together

Ludwig Steven Cox

Copyright © 2025 Ludwig Steven Cox. All rights reserved.

No part of this publication may be reproduced, distributed, or transmitted in any form or by any means, including photocopying, recording, or other electronic or mechanical methods, without the prior written permission of the copyright holder, except in the case of brief quotations embodied in critical reviews and certain other noncommercial uses permitted by copyright law.

First Edition

Paperback ISBN: 9781923604438

This book is for informational and educational purposes only and is not intended as a substitute for professional medical, psychological, or therapeutic advice, diagnosis, or treatment. The content reflects the author's personal experiences and research but should not be considered professional medical or psychological guidance.

The information presented is based on general principles and may not apply to every individual situation. Readers are encouraged to consult with qualified healthcare professionals, licensed therapists, or medical practitioners before making decisions about their mental health, medical care, or treatment options.

Names, characters, places, and incidents referenced in examples throughout this book are either products of the author's imagination or are used in a purely illustrative context. Any resemblance to actual persons, living or deceased, or actual events is purely coincidental. No real individuals are identified by name except where explicitly noted as public figures or published sources.

The author and publisher disclaim any liability arising directly or indirectly from the use of this book. Results may vary for each individual, and no outcomes are guaranteed.

If you are experiencing a mental health emergency, please contact emergency services or a crisis hotline immediately.

Chapter 1: The Moment Everything Makes Sense

Understanding Your AuDHD Discovery

Have you ever felt like you were living two different lives inside one body? One part of you craves routine and predictability, while another part gets restless and seeks novelty. You might find yourself meticulously organizing your workspace, then abandoning the system entirely when it feels too constraining. Or perhaps you've noticed how you can hyperfocus on fascinating topics for hours, yet struggle to complete mundane tasks that others seem to handle effortlessly.

If these contradictions feel familiar, you're not alone. Millions of adults are discovering that their lifelong experience of internal conflict actually has a name: **AuDHD** – the co-occurrence of autism and ADHD in the same person. This isn't just having two separate conditions; it's experiencing a unique neurological profile where autism and ADHD interact in complex, sometimes contradictory ways.

For many people, learning about AuDHD brings an overwhelming sense of recognition. Suddenly, the internal battles that have shaped their entire lives begin to make sense. The exhaustion from masking autism traits while simultaneously managing ADHD symptoms becomes understandable. The confusion about why traditional coping strategies never quite worked becomes clear.

What AuDHD Really Means

When most people think about autism and ADHD together, they imagine someone who simply has both conditions separately. But **AuDHD represents something far more complex – it's about how**

these two neurotypes interact and influence each other within the same nervous system.

Think of it this way: if your brain were a sophisticated sound system, autism might be the component that prefers consistent, high-quality input with minimal interference. ADHD, meanwhile, might be the component that constantly scans for new, interesting signals and gets bored with repetitive input. When both components operate in the same system, they create a unique output that's different from either one alone.

This interaction explains why traditional autism resources might feel partially helpful but not completely applicable. It also explains why ADHD strategies sometimes work brilliantly for a while, then suddenly stop being effective. **You're not failing at being autistic or ADHD – you're succeeding at being AuDHD, which is its own distinct experience.**

The Dance of Contradictions

People with AuDHD often describe feeling like they're constantly negotiating between opposing needs. You might find yourself in these seemingly contradictory situations:

- Craving both routine and spontaneity
- Needing detailed planning while also working best under pressure
- Seeking sensory input in some areas while avoiding it in others
- Wanting social connection but finding social situations exhausting
- Having intense interests that shift and change over time
- Feeling both understimulated and overwhelmed simultaneously

These aren't character flaws or signs of confusion – **they're the natural result of having two different neurological operating systems that sometimes want different things**. Understanding this can be profoundly liberating because it means you can stop trying to force yourself into a single category and start working with your unique neurological makeup.

Why Diagnosis Often Comes Late

The path to AuDHD recognition is rarely straightforward. Many adults discover this aspect of themselves decades into their lives, often feeling frustrated about the lost time and missed opportunities for understanding. But this delay isn't accidental – there are systemic reasons why AuDHD often goes unrecognized for years.

The Masking Effect

One of the primary reasons AuDHD goes unnoticed is the phenomenon of masking. **Masking occurs when you unconsciously or consciously suppress your natural responses and behaviors to blend in with neurotypical expectations**. For people with AuDHD, this process becomes particularly complex because you're masking two different sets of traits that might even mask each other.

Consider someone who has learned to appear socially engaged by asking lots of questions and showing animated interest (masking autistic social differences), while simultaneously using this social stimulation to manage ADHD's need for engagement. From the outside, this person might appear naturally sociable and confident. Inside, they might be working incredibly hard to maintain this presentation while managing sensory overload and social exhaustion.

The energy required for this level of masking is enormous, which is why many people describe feeling utterly exhausted after social interactions, even positive ones. **You're not antisocial or defective – you're managing a complex neurological balancing act that most people never even notice.**

Gender Bias in Recognition

Traditional understanding of both autism and ADHD has been heavily influenced by studies of young boys, creating diagnostic criteria that often miss how these conditions present in girls, women, and gender-diverse individuals. This bias becomes compounded when both conditions are present.

Women with AuDHD might develop sophisticated masking strategies early in life, learning to mimic social behaviors while channeling their intense interests into socially acceptable areas. They might appear to be high achievers who "have it all together," while internally struggling with executive function challenges, sensory sensitivities, and social exhaustion.

The hyperactive presentation of ADHD, which is more easily recognized, might be suppressed in favor of the inattentive type, especially when combined with autism's tendency toward internalized experiences. **This means that many women and gender-diverse individuals spend years being misunderstood as anxious, depressed, or simply "sensitive," rather than receiving accurate understanding of their neurological differences.**

Overlapping and Contradictory Traits

Another significant factor in delayed recognition is how autism and ADHD traits can appear to cancel each other out or create confusing presentations. Mental health professionals might see someone who has periods of intense focus (assuming this rules out ADHD) without recognizing that this represents autistic special interests combined with ADHD hyperfocus.

Similarly, someone might appear disorganized and scattered in some areas (ADHD traits) while being extremely methodical and precise in others (autistic traits). This inconsistency can be puzzling to professionals who are looking for clear, consistent patterns rather than the complex interplay of two different neurological styles.

The result is that many people receive partial diagnoses, incomplete understanding, or are told they don't quite fit any particular category. This can lead to years of self-doubt and confusion about why recommended strategies only work sometimes or why they feel different from others who share their diagnoses.

The Paradox Puzzle: How Autism and ADHD Mask Each Other

Understanding how autism and ADHD interact requires recognizing that they don't simply coexist – they influence each other in ways that can make both conditions less obvious to outside observers and sometimes even to yourself.

The Organization Paradox

Many people with AuDHD develop what appears to be strong organizational systems, leading others (and sometimes themselves) to assume they don't struggle with executive function. However, these systems often serve a dual purpose: they provide the predictable structure that autism craves while creating external scaffolding for ADHD's executive function challenges.

When these systems break down – which they inevitably do because they're often overly complex or rigid – the person might experience a cascade effect where both their need for order and their executive function abilities become compromised simultaneously. **This isn't failure; it's the natural result of trying to meet two different sets of neurological needs with a single system.**

The Social Energy Contradiction

People with AuDHD often confuse themselves and others with their social presentation. They might appear highly social and engaging during certain periods, then seem to withdraw completely. This happens because ADHD's need for stimulation might drive social seeking, while autism's social processing differences create exhaustion from these same interactions.

You might find yourself drawn to social situations for the engagement and stimulation they provide, then feeling overwhelmed by the unpredictability and social demands. **This creates a push-pull dynamic where you simultaneously crave and avoid social** connection, leading to confusion about your "true" social preferences.

The Interest Intensity Balance

Special interests – those deeply absorbing topics or activities that capture complete attention – present differently in AuDHD than in autism alone. While autistic special interests tend to be stable and long-lasting, ADHD's novelty-seeking can create a pattern where interests are incredibly intense but shift over time.

This might look like someone who becomes completely absorbed in learning everything about a particular topic, develops genuine expertise, then gradually shifts focus to something entirely different. **Rather than indicating lack of commitment or follow-through, this pattern represents the intersection of autistic depth and ADHD's need for novelty.**

Common Pathways to Discovery

Most adults don't stumble upon AuDHD information randomly. There are several common experiences that lead people to recognize this aspect of themselves, each reflecting different aspects of how AuDHD shows up in adult life.

The Burnout Revelation

One of the most frequent paths to AuDHD discovery begins with burnout – not just everyday stress or work fatigue, but a profound exhaustion that affects every aspect of functioning. This burnout often happens when the systems and strategies you've developed to manage daily life finally become unsustainable.

You might find yourself unable to maintain the level of masking and coping that previously worked. Simple tasks become overwhelming, social interactions feel impossible, and the internal resources you've always relied on seem depleted. **This isn't personal failure – it's your nervous system signaling that the current approach isn't sustainable long-term.**

During burnout recovery, many people start researching their symptoms and stumble upon information about autism, ADHD, or both. The recognition often begins with small details – reading about sensory sensitivities and realizing you've always avoided certain textures, or learning about executive function differences and recognizing your own patterns of organization and struggle.

The Child's Diagnosis Connection

Another common discovery path occurs when someone's child receives an autism or ADHD diagnosis. As parents learn about these conditions to support their children, they begin recognizing similar patterns in their own lives. This recognition often brings a mixture of understanding and grief – relief at finally having explanations, combined with sadness about years of self-misunderstanding.

The family connection to neurodiversity can be particularly illuminating because it provides context for traits that might have been dismissed as personality quirks or character flaws. **Seeing these traits as neurological differences rather than personal shortcomings can be profoundly healing.**

The Social Media Recognition

In recent years, social media has become a significant pathway to AuDHD discovery. Platforms like TikTok and Instagram feature content creators sharing their experiences with autism and ADHD, often describing specific scenarios that resonate deeply with viewers.

You might watch a video about masking behaviors and suddenly recognize your own patterns, or see someone describe their sensory experiences in words you've never heard but that perfectly capture your own reality. **These moments of recognition can be powerful because they're often the first time you realize that other people share your specific experiences.**

The Crisis Catalyst

Sometimes AuDHD discovery happens during major life transitions or crises – divorce, job loss, death of a family member, or other significant changes. These situations often disrupt established coping mechanisms and reveal underlying patterns that were previously masked by routine and structure.

During crisis periods, the extra demands on your system might make it impossible to maintain usual masking behaviors, leading others (or yourself) to notice traits that were previously hidden. **While these discoveries during difficult times can feel overwhelming, they often provide crucial insights that lead to better self-understanding and support.**

Validation: Your Struggles Were Real

Perhaps the most important aspect of AuDHD discovery is the validation it provides for experiences that might have been minimized, dismissed, or misunderstood throughout your life. **Learning about AuDHD doesn't mean you're suddenly different – it means you finally have accurate language for who you've always been.**

The Relief of Explanation

Many people describe their AuDHD discovery as feeling like puzzle pieces finally clicking into place. Behaviors that seemed random or problematic suddenly make sense within a neurological context. The exhaustion you felt after social events, the way you organized and reorganized your living space, the intensity of your interests, the difficulty with certain types of tasks – all of these experiences gain new meaning.

This doesn't mean everything becomes easy once you understand AuDHD, but it does mean you can stop blaming yourself for neurological differences that are simply part of how your brain works. **You weren't being difficult, oversensitive, or lazy – you were navigating life with a different neurological operating system.**

Reframing Past Experiences

AuDHD discovery often leads to a process of reframing past experiences through a new lens. Situations where you felt like you were failing or not measuring up can be understood as mismatches between your neurological needs and environmental demands, rather than personal shortcomings.

That job where you couldn't focus despite your best efforts? It might have involved tasks that didn't align with how your AuDHD brain processes information. The social situations where you felt awkward and drained? They might have required types of social processing that are genuinely more challenging for your neurotype.

This reframing isn't about making excuses – it's about developing accurate understanding that allows for better self-advocacy and more effective strategies going forward.

Permission to Be Yourself

One of the most profound aspects of AuDHD recognition is that it provides permission to stop trying to be neurotypical and start working with your actual neurological makeup. This might mean acknowledging that certain environments are genuinely more challenging for you, that you need different types of rest and recovery, or that your way of processing information has both strengths and challenges.

You might realize that the parts of yourself you've tried to hide or change are actually adaptive responses to having a different type of nervous system. **The goal isn't to become neurotypical – it's to understand and work with your AuDHD brain in ways that support your wellbeing and effectiveness.**

Self-Assessment: Which Traits Masked Which?

Understanding your personal AuDHD experience requires examining how your autism and ADHD traits have interacted throughout your life. This self-assessment can help you identify patterns and begin understanding your unique neurological profile.

Sensory Processing Patterns

Consider how you respond to different types of sensory input. You might notice that:

- You seek certain types of sensory input (ADHD) while avoiding others (autism)
- Your sensory preferences change based on your energy level or stress
- You have elaborate systems for managing your sensory environment
- You're drawn to situations that provide the "right" amount of sensory input

Reflect on how these patterns have shaped your choices in living spaces, clothing, food, social environments, and work situations.

Attention and Focus Dynamics

Examine your relationship with attention and focus by considering:

- Topics or activities that capture your complete attention for extended periods
- Situations where you struggle to focus despite wanting to engage
- The difference between chosen focus (special interests) and required focus (assigned tasks)
- How your attention patterns have affected your academic and professional experiences

Notice how your ability to focus might be excellent in some areas while being challenging in others, rather than being consistently strong or weak.

Social Energy Management

Reflect on your social experiences by exploring:

- Situations where social interaction feels energizing versus draining
- The difference between social situations you choose versus those you're required to attend
- Your strategies for managing social demands and expectations
- How your social presentation might differ from your internal experience

Consider how you might have developed sophisticated social skills that mask underlying challenges with social processing and energy management.

Timeline Exercise: Reframing Life Events Through AuDHD Lens

This exercise involves examining key life events and experiences through the perspective of your AuDHD understanding. Rather than focusing on what went wrong, this approach helps identify patterns and recognize adaptive strategies you may have developed.

Early Years Recognition

Look back at your childhood and adolescent experiences with fresh perspective:

- Intense interests that others found unusual or excessive
- Social situations that felt confusing or overwhelming
- Learning environments where you excelled versus struggled
- Sensory preferences and aversions that shaped your choices
- Ways you learned to navigate social expectations

Rather than judging these experiences as positive or negative, consider how they reflect your brain's attempts to meet its neurological needs within available environments.

Educational Patterns

Examine your educational experiences for AuDHD-related patterns:

- Subjects that captured your complete interest versus those you couldn't engage with
- Teaching styles that worked well for you versus those that felt impossible
- Social aspects of school that were energizing versus exhausting
- Organizational systems that helped versus hindered your success
- Times when you felt misunderstood by teachers or peers

Consider how your academic performance might have reflected the match between your learning style and educational approaches, rather than your intelligence or effort.

Professional Journey

Review your work experiences through an AuDHD lens:

- Jobs or roles where you felt energized and capable versus drained and overwhelmed
- Work environments that supported versus challenged your sensory needs
- Projects that allowed deep focus versus those requiring constant task-switching
- Interpersonal dynamics that felt natural versus those requiring significant energy
- Times when you received feedback that felt confusing or inconsistent

Notice how your professional satisfaction might correlate with how well different roles aligned with your AuDHD traits and needs.

Quick Wins: Immediate Relief Strategies

While understanding AuDHD is a long-term process, there are immediate strategies that can provide relief and support your wellbeing as you navigate this new understanding.

Energy Management Fundamentals

Start recognizing and respecting your energy patterns:

- **Track your energy levels** throughout different activities and environments
- **Identify your optimal times** for different types of tasks
- **Build in recovery time** after socially or cognitively demanding activities
- **Create transition rituals** to help your brain shift between different types of activities

These strategies acknowledge that your energy management might be more complex than neurotypical patterns, requiring more intentional planning and self-advocacy.

Sensory Environment Optimization

Make immediate improvements to your sensory environment:

- **Adjust lighting** to levels that feel comfortable and supportive
- **Consider sound management** through noise-canceling headphones or background music
- **Optimize your workspace** for your specific sensory preferences
- **Choose clothing and fabrics** that feel comfortable throughout the day

Small changes to your sensory environment can have significant impacts on your comfort and functioning.

Social Boundary Setting

Begin establishing social boundaries that support your wellbeing:

- **Practice saying no** to social commitments that don't align with your energy
- **Communicate your needs** clearly rather than trying to mask or accommodate
- **Create scripts** for common social situations that feel challenging
- **Build in alone time** before and after social activities

Setting boundaries isn't selfish – it's essential self-care that allows you to show up more authentically in your relationships.

Information Processing Support

Develop systems that support your unique information processing style:

- **Break large tasks** into smaller, manageable components
- **Use visual organization** methods like charts, lists, or digital tools
- **Create external memory systems** to support executive function
- **Allow processing time** for important decisions or complex information

These strategies work with your brain's natural patterns rather than fighting against them.

Understanding Your Path Forward

Discovering AuDHD is rarely the end of a journey – it's usually the beginning of a new phase of self-understanding and intentional living. **This recognition provides a foundation for making choices that align with your neurological reality rather than fighting against it.**

As you continue to explore what AuDHD means for your specific experience, remember that this understanding is meant to be empowering rather than limiting. **You're not broken and you don't need to be fixed – you need accurate information and strategies that work with your brain's natural patterns.**

The process of integrating this new understanding takes time and patience with yourself. Some days the insights will feel liberating and exciting; other days they might bring up grief or frustration about missed opportunities or misunderstandings. Both responses are completely normal and valid parts of the discovery process.

Most importantly, remember that understanding AuDHD is about addition, not subtraction. You're not losing parts of yourself or discovering limitations – you're gaining vocabulary for strengths and challenges you've always had, and tools for navigating life more effectively.

As we turn to the next area of exploration, we'll examine the emotional aspects of late discovery and the grief process that many people experience when they recognize how long they've been misunderstood, even by themselves. This emotional processing is a crucial part of integrating your AuDHD understanding and building a foundation for authentic living.

Chapter 2: The Grief No One Talks About

Processing Loss, Finding Peace

Learning about your AuDHD often brings an unexpected emotional response that catches many people off guard. You might expect relief, validation, or excitement about finally having answers. While these feelings often come, they're frequently accompanied by something more complex and harder to name: **grief**.

This grief isn't talked about enough in neurodivergent communities, perhaps because it feels contradictory to celebrate neurodiversity while simultaneously mourning aspects of the neurodivergent experience. But grief and acceptance aren't opposites – **they're often different stages of the same healing process**.

The grief that accompanies late AuDHD discovery is unique and multifaceted. It's not like grieving the loss of a person or even the end of a relationship. It's more like grieving a version of yourself and your life story that you're now realizing never quite existed in the first place. You're mourning opportunities that weren't available because your needs weren't understood, relationships that might have been different with better communication, and decades of energy spent trying to fit into spaces that weren't designed for your type of brain.

This grief is valid, necessary, and ultimately healing. It's not a sign that you're ungrateful for your neurodivergent traits or that you wish you were neurotypical. It's a natural response to recognizing how much energy you've spent adapting to a world that didn't understand your needs, and how much of your authentic self you've kept hidden to survive in environments that weren't designed for you.

The Five Stages of Late-Diagnosis Grief

While grief is highly individual, many people who discover their AuDHD in adulthood experience recognizable stages that mirror but differ from traditional grief models. Understanding these stages can help normalize your experience and recognize that what you're feeling is a natural part of the discovery process.

Stage 1: Shock and Recognition

The initial stage often involves a sense of shock, even when the discovery feels positive. You might find yourself thinking, "How did I not know this about myself for so long?" or "How did everyone miss this?" This stage can involve rapid recognition of patterns – suddenly seeing your entire life through a new lens and having experiences make sense in ways they never did before.

During this stage, many people experience what feels like a mental catalog update, where memories and experiences are rapidly re-categorized under this new understanding. **The shock isn't necessarily negative – it can feel like finally solving a puzzle that's been missing pieces for decades.** But it can also feel overwhelming to have so much of your self-understanding shift simultaneously.

You might find yourself reaching out to friends and family, explaining your discovery and asking if they noticed these traits. Sometimes their responses validate your recognition; other times they express surprise or even skepticism, which can intensify feelings of confusion about your own experience.

Stage 2: Relief and Validation

As the initial shock settles, many people experience profound relief. **Finally having language for experiences that felt inexplicable can be incredibly validating.** You might feel lighter, like you can stop blaming yourself for struggles that you now understand as neurological differences rather than personal failings.

This stage often involves voracious consumption of information about AuDHD – reading everything available, watching videos, joining online communities, and seeking out others who share similar experiences. **This information seeking isn't obsessive behavior; it's your brain trying to build a comprehensive understanding of itself.**

The relief can feel so intense that some people want to share their discovery with everyone, explaining their newfound understanding to anyone who will listen. This enthusiasm is natural and healthy, though it's worth being prepared for mixed reactions from others who might not immediately understand the significance of your discovery.

Stage 3: Anger at Missed Opportunities

After the relief settles, anger often emerges. This anger can be directed in multiple directions: at educational systems that didn't recognize your needs, at healthcare providers who missed signs, at family members who dismissed your struggles, and sometimes at yourself for not figuring it out sooner.

This anger is particularly complex because it's not anger at having AuDHD – it's anger at how the world's lack of understanding affected your life. You might feel frustrated about accommodations that could have made school easier, support that could have made relationships healthier, or self-understanding that could have prevented years of self-blame.

Some people feel angry at the messaging they received about their traits – being called "too sensitive," "weird," "antisocial," or "lazy" when they were actually demonstrating neurological differences. **This anger often represents your healthy recognition that you deserved better understanding and support.**

It's important to acknowledge this anger without letting it consume your energy indefinitely. The anger serves a purpose – it helps you recognize that your struggles were real and that better support should have been available. But it's most useful when it motivates self-advocacy and system change rather than rumination about the past.

Stage 4: Bargaining with "What If" Scenarios

The bargaining stage in AuDHD grief often involves extensive "what if" thinking. What if you had known about this in college? What if your parents had understood? What if you had received appropriate accommodations at work? What if you hadn't spent so much energy masking your authentic self?

This stage can be particularly intense because unlike other types of grief, you're mourning possibilities rather than concrete losses. You're imagining alternative life paths that might have unfolded with better understanding, different support, or earlier recognition of your neurological differences.

While some amount of this thinking is natural and even useful for identifying what you want to change going forward, it can become problematic when it prevents you from engaging with your current reality. **The goal isn't to eliminate these thoughts but to recognize them as part of the grief process while continuing to invest energy in creating the life you want now.**

Stage 5: Integration and Acceptance

The final stage involves integrating your AuDHD understanding into your overall sense of self and moving forward with this knowledge. This doesn't mean you'll never feel sad about missed opportunities or frustrated with lack of understanding from others. **Integration means that your AuDHD identity becomes one important part of your self-concept rather than consuming your entire identity.**

During this stage, you might find yourself naturally advocating for better understanding in your communities, seeking out relationships with other neurodivergent people, and making life changes that better align with your neurological needs. **The energy that was previously spent on grief becomes available for creating positive change.**

Integration also involves developing a more nuanced understanding of your AuDHD experience – recognizing both challenges and strengths, understanding how it affects different areas of your life, and learning to communicate your needs effectively to others.

Mourning the Life That Could Have Been

One of the most complex aspects of AuDHD grief involves mourning a life that you never actually lived but can now imagine might have been possible with different circumstances. **This isn't about regretting your current life, but rather acknowledging the additional challenges you faced due to lack of understanding and support.**

Educational Opportunities

Many people find themselves grieving educational experiences that could have been different with proper understanding. Perhaps you struggled in traditional classroom settings but were never offered alternative learning approaches that might have worked better for your AuDHD brain. You might imagine how different your academic confidence would have been with teachers who understood your needs rather than viewing your differences as behavioral problems.

This grief often involves recognizing how much additional energy you spent trying to succeed in environments that weren't designed for your learning style. You might have been labeled as unmotivated or having "potential that you're not living up to," when actually you were working twice as hard as your peers to achieve the same results in systems that didn't accommodate your neurological differences.

Some people feel sadness about career paths that might have been available with different educational experiences, or wonder how their relationship with learning itself might have been different with early understanding and support.

Relationship Possibilities

AuDHD discovery often brings awareness of how your neurological differences affected your relationships, leading to grief about connections that might have been deeper or more authentic with better understanding. You might recognize patterns where you masked your authentic self to maintain relationships, or where communication difficulties led to misunderstandings that could have been prevented.

This grief isn't about blaming yourself or others for past relationship challenges – it's about acknowledging how lack of

awareness affected your ability to be authentic in relationships. You might feel sad about friendships that ended due to misunderstandings about your social needs, romantic relationships where your sensory sensitivities weren't respected, or family dynamics that involved criticism of traits that were actually neurological differences.

Some people feel grief about not having had neurodivergent community earlier in life, wondering how different their sense of belonging might have been with access to others who shared similar experiences.

Career and Professional Development

Professional life often becomes a significant focus of AuDHD grief, as many people recognize how their career paths were shaped by accommodating neurotypical work environments rather than seeking roles that aligned with their strengths and needs. **You might feel sadness about jobs you stayed in too long because you assumed the difficulties were personal failings rather than environmental mismatches.**

This grief often includes recognizing opportunities you didn't pursue because you didn't understand your own capabilities and needs. Perhaps you avoided leadership roles because you thought you were "bad with people," when actually you just needed different communication strategies. Or you might have left careers that interested you because the sensory environment was overwhelming, not realizing that accommodations might have been possible.

Some people feel grief about the energy that went into masking in professional environments – energy that could have been directed toward creative work, skill development, or career advancement if they had better understood their needs and been able to advocate for appropriate support.

Anger at Missed Opportunities and Misunderstandings

The anger that emerges during AuDHD grief processing is often intense and multidirectional. **This anger serves important purposes**

– it validates that your struggles were real, that you deserved better support, and that systemic failures affected your life in significant ways. Understanding the different aspects of this anger can help you process it constructively rather than letting it become destructive.

Systemic Failures

Much of the anger that emerges relates to systems that failed to recognize and support neurodivergent needs. Educational systems that pathologized differences rather than accommodating them, healthcare systems that missed obvious signs, and workplace cultures that demanded conformity rather than celebrating diverse strengths.

This anger is justified and important because it recognizes that individual struggles often reflect systemic problems rather than personal failings. You might feel angry that autism and ADHD research historically focused on young boys, leading to diagnostic criteria that missed how these conditions present in other populations. Or you might feel frustrated that masking was so effective that it prevented recognition of your support needs.

This systemic anger can be channeled constructively through advocacy work, supporting organizations that promote neurodivergent awareness, or simply refusing to accept inadequate treatment in your current interactions with these systems.

Family and Relationship Dynamics

Anger often emerges regarding family members or friends who dismissed your struggles or pressured you to "just try harder" when you were already working at capacity. **This anger can be particularly complex when it involves people who love you but lacked the understanding to provide appropriate support.**

You might feel angry about being called "dramatic" for sensory sensitivities, "antisocial" for needing alone time, or "lazy" for executive function challenges. These labels not only failed to provide helpful support but actively worked against your self-understanding and self-acceptance.

Processing this anger doesn't require forgiveness or maintaining relationships that continue to be harmful. It does involve recognizing that these responses often reflected others' lack of knowledge rather than intentional cruelty, while still validating that the impact on you was real and significant.

Self-Directed Frustration

Many people experience anger directed at themselves – frustration about not recognizing their AuDHD sooner, anger about years of self-blame and harsh self-criticism, or frustration about accommodating others' misunderstandings of their needs.

This self-directed anger often needs the most compassionate attention because it continues patterns of self-blame that may have been present for years. It's important to recognize that not knowing about AuDHD doesn't reflect personal failure – it reflects limited awareness and representation in mainstream understanding of neurodiversity.

You did the best you could with the information and support that were available to you. **The fact that you're now seeking better understanding and support demonstrates strength and self-advocacy, not failure.**

The "Parade of Embarrassing Memories" Phenomenon

One of the most challenging aspects of AuDHD grief involves what many people describe as a "parade of embarrassing memories" – situations from throughout your life that now make sense as AuDHD-related experiences rather than social failures or character flaws. **This recontextualization can be both relieving and painful.**

Reframing Social Difficulties

You might suddenly understand why certain social situations felt so difficult or why you seemed to miss social cues that others picked up easily. Conversations where you talked too long about your special interests, social events where you felt completely overwhelmed, or times when you inadvertently offended someone by being too direct or honest.

These memories can feel embarrassing when viewed through your old self-understanding, but they take on different meaning when understood as neurological differences rather than social failures. The challenge is developing compassion for your past self while integrating this new understanding.

Rather than feeling ashamed of these memories, you can recognize them as evidence of your brain working differently, not defectively. **Your past self was doing the best they could with the tools and understanding available at the time.**

Academic and Professional Moments

You might remember times when you struggled to complete assignments that seemed easy for others, couldn't focus during meetings or lectures, or had difficulty with organizational systems that worked well for your peers. These memories can feel particularly painful because they often led to criticism or negative evaluations that affected your opportunities and self-concept.

Understanding these experiences as AuDHD-related rather than personal failings can be profoundly healing, but it also brings awareness of how much additional challenge you faced without appropriate support. This awareness is part of what makes the grief process necessary and valuable.

Family and Relationship Interactions

Family memories often feature prominently in this recontextualization process. You might remember being overwhelmed at family gatherings, having meltdowns that were treated as behavioral problems, or feeling like you never quite fit in with family dynamics despite genuine love and connection.

These memories highlight how your neurological differences affected your relationships from an early age, often in ways that weren't understood by anyone involved. Processing these memories with compassion for both yourself and your family members can be challenging but ultimately healing.

Moving from Grief to Integration

The goal of processing AuDHD-related grief isn't to eliminate all sadness about missed opportunities or frustration with past misunderstandings. **The goal is to process these emotions thoroughly enough that they don't prevent you from creating the life you want going forward.**

Honoring Your Resilience

Part of moving through grief involves recognizing the incredible resilience you demonstrated throughout your life. **You navigated educational, social, and professional environments that weren't designed for your neurological differences, often without understanding why these environments felt so challenging.**

You developed coping strategies, found ways to contribute your unique strengths, and maintained relationships despite communication differences and energy management challenges. **This isn't just survival – it's evidence of remarkable adaptability and strength.**

Recognizing your resilience doesn't minimize the additional challenges you faced or the support you should have received. **It acknowledges that you've already demonstrated the strength and creativity necessary to build a life that better aligns with your AuDHD needs.**

Creating Meaning from Experience

Many people find that their AuDHD discovery and subsequent grief processing leads to deeper empathy for others who are struggling with unrecognized differences. **Your experience of being misunderstood can become a source of compassion and support for others who are facing similar challenges.**

This doesn't mean you need to become an advocate or educator if that doesn't align with your interests and energy. But many people find that their difficult experiences gain additional meaning when they can be used to support others or create positive change in their communities.

Building Forward-Focused Identity

Integration involves developing an identity that acknowledges your AuDHD experience while not being entirely defined by it. **You are a complex person with many interests, relationships, strengths, and goals – AuDHD is one important aspect of who you are, but it's not the only aspect.**

This balanced perspective allows you to advocate for your needs and seek appropriate support without feeling like your entire life needs to revolve around managing neurological differences. **It also allows you to appreciate the unique strengths and perspectives that come with your AuDHD brain while acknowledging areas where you need additional support.**

Grief Processing Framework Specific to AuDHD

Traditional grief counseling approaches may not fully address the unique aspects of neurodivergent grief. **This framework is designed specifically for processing the complex emotions that accompany late AuDHD discovery.**

Step 1: Validation Without Judgment

Begin by acknowledging that all of your emotions about your AuDHD discovery are valid, including emotions that might seem contradictory. It's possible to feel grateful for understanding while also feeling angry about missed support, or to appreciate your neurological differences while also grieving the additional challenges they created.

Write down or speak aloud the emotions you're experiencing without trying to justify them or make them more logical. Grief isn't logical, and trying to make it logical often prevents thorough processing.

Step 2: Contextualize Your Experience

Research the broader context of AuDHD awareness and recognition. Understanding that your late discovery is part of a larger pattern affecting millions of people can help reduce self-blame and isolation. **You're not uniquely oblivious or delayed – you're part of a generation that's gaining access to information that wasn't previously available.**

This contextualization can help direct anger toward systemic issues rather than personal failings, which is both more accurate and more productive for long-term healing.

Step 3: Rewrite Your Personal Narrative

Consciously work to rewrite your life story with AuDHD understanding integrated throughout. This doesn't mean everything becomes positive or that all challenges disappear from your narrative. **It means that difficulties are understood as interactions between your neurological differences and environmental factors rather than as evidence of personal deficiency.**

This rewriting process often takes time and may involve working with a neurodivergent-affirming therapist who understands the unique aspects of late neurodivergent discovery.

Step 4: Develop Future-Focused Goals

Channel your grief processing energy into creating specific, achievable goals that align with your AuDHD understanding. This might involve seeking accommodations at work, ending relationships that require extensive masking, or pursuing interests that you previously thought were "too intense" or "weird."

The goal isn't to completely restructure your life immediately, but to begin making choices that align with your authentic needs and preferences rather than trying to fit neurotypical expectations.

Step 5: Build Community Connection

Seek out relationships with others who understand neurodivergent experiences, whether through online communities, local support groups, or friendships with other neurodivergent people. **Community connection can provide validation, practical strategies, and the experience of being understood without extensive explanation.**

This doesn't mean you need to abandon neurotypical relationships, but having access to neurodivergent community can provide a different type of understanding and support that may have been missing from your life.

Self-Compassion Scripts for Difficult Memories

When processing painful memories through your new AuDHD understanding, having specific language for self-compassion can be helpful. **These scripts provide alternatives to the self-critical language that may have been your default for years.**

For Social Misunderstandings

"I was doing my best to connect and communicate with the tools and understanding I had at the time. My brain processes social information differently, and that's not a character flaw. I deserved patience and understanding, and I can give that to myself now."

For Academic or Professional Struggles

"I was working twice as hard as my peers to succeed in systems that weren't designed for my type of brain. My struggles reflected environmental mismatches, not lack of intelligence or effort. I have unique strengths that deserve recognition and support."

For Masking and Authenticity

"I learned to mask my authentic self as a survival strategy in environments that didn't understand or accept neurodivergent traits. This showed incredible adaptability and strength. I can now choose when and how to share my authentic self with people who earn that trust."

For Family and Relationship Challenges

"I was navigating relationships without understanding my own needs and communication style. This made connection more difficult, but it doesn't reflect my worth as a person or my capacity for meaningful relationships. I can build healthier relationships now with better self-understanding."

These scripts aren't meant to eliminate all difficult emotions, but to provide gentler alternatives to harsh self-criticism while you process complex feelings about your past experiences.

Building upon these insights, we can begin to explore the unique ways your AuDHD brain operates and the specific strategies that can support your success and wellbeing. Understanding the grief process creates space for appreciating the remarkable complexity and capability of your neurological differences, setting the foundation for working with rather than against your brain's natural patterns.

Chapter 3: Understanding Your Unique Brain

The AuDHD Operating System

Think of your brain as running a sophisticated operating system – one that processes information, manages resources, and responds to environmental input in ways that are both highly effective and beautifully complex. **Most people are running what we might call the "neurotypical OS," but you're running something entirely different: the AuDHD system.**

This isn't a flawed or inferior system – it's a different architecture entirely, with its own logic, strengths, and resource requirements. **Understanding how your particular system works is the key to optimizing its performance and working with its natural patterns rather than fighting against them.**

The challenge many people with AuDHD face is that they've spent years trying to run neurotypical software on their AuDHD hardware, wondering why everything feels more difficult and exhausting than it seems to be for others. **It's not that you're doing anything wrong – you're just using strategies designed for a different type of system.**

When you understand your unique operating system, everything changes. Tasks that felt impossible become manageable when approached in AuDHD-compatible ways. Environments that felt overwhelming become tolerable with appropriate adjustments. **Most importantly, you can stop blaming yourself for your brain's resource requirements and start working with them strategically.**

This understanding doesn't eliminate all challenges, but it transforms them from mysterious personal failings into predictable system requirements that can be planned for and accommodated.

How Autism and ADHD Interact (Not Cancel Out)

One of the most important aspects of understanding AuDHD is recognizing that autism and ADHD don't simply coexist in your brain – **they interact in complex ways that create a unique neurological profile different from either condition alone.**

Many people mistakenly assume that autism and ADHD traits would cancel each other out, thinking that ADHD's hyperactivity would eliminate autism's need for calm, or that autism's desire for routine would cure ADHD's restlessness. In reality, **both sets of traits remain active, creating a brain that needs to satisfy sometimes competing requirements simultaneously.**

The Interaction Model

Instead of cancellation, think of autism and ADHD as two different software programs running simultaneously on your brain's hardware. Sometimes they work together harmoniously, sometimes they compete for resources, and sometimes one temporarily dominates while the other runs in the background.

For example, your autistic brain might crave deep focus on a special interest, while your ADHD brain provides the intensity and passion that makes that focus possible. This creates periods of hyperfocus that are more sustained and productive than typical ADHD hyperfocus alone.

Alternatively, your autism might need predictable routine while your ADHD craves novelty and stimulation. Rather than these canceling out, you might find yourself creating routines that incorporate variety, or establishing patterns that provide stability while allowing for spontaneous elements within structured timeframes.

Amplification Effects

Sometimes autism and ADHD traits amplify each other rather than competing. **Sensory sensitivities from autism combined with ADHD's alertness to environmental changes can create a heightened awareness system that's both highly perceptive and easily overwhelmed.**

This amplification can be a strength – you might notice details and patterns that others miss, pick up on subtle environmental changes, or have unusually strong intuitive responses to people and situations. **But it can also mean that sensory overload happens more quickly and intensely than it would with either condition alone.**

Similarly, the combination of autistic special interests and ADHD's intensity can create expertise that develops rapidly and deeply. **You might find yourself becoming genuinely expert in areas that capture your interest, combining autism's systematic approach with ADHD's passionate engagement.**

Masking Interactions

One of the most complex interactions involves how masking behaviors from autism can hide ADHD symptoms, and vice versa. **You might have learned to appear calm and controlled (masking ADHD hyperactivity) while using internal stimming or mental activity to manage your sensory and attention needs (accommodating autism).**

Or you might present as socially engaged and spontaneous (masking autistic social differences) while using this social interaction as stimulation for your ADHD brain. **From the outside, you might appear neurotypical, while internally you're working incredibly hard to balance competing neurological needs.**

Understanding these masking interactions is crucial because it explains why you might feel exhausted after situations that others find energizing, or why strategies that work for autism-only or ADHD-only individuals don't quite work for you.

The Push-Pull of Opposing Needs

Living with AuDHD often feels like being caught between opposing forces, each representing legitimate neurological needs that deserve attention. **Learning to navigate these opposing needs without judgment is essential for developing sustainable life strategies.**

Routine Versus Novelty

Your autistic brain might crave routine, predictability, and familiar patterns that provide security and reduce cognitive load. **Simultaneously, your ADHD brain might feel restless and understimulated by too much routine, needing novelty and change to maintain engagement and motivation.**

This creates what many people describe as a constant internal negotiation. You might find yourself establishing routines that feel comforting, then feeling trapped by them and needing to break free. **Or you might avoid routine entirely to satisfy your ADHD needs, then feel anxious and overwhelmed by the lack of predictable structure.**

The solution isn't choosing one need over the other – it's finding ways to satisfy both simultaneously. This might mean creating flexible routines that provide structure while allowing for spontaneous elements, or establishing rituals around change itself.

Stimulation Seeking Versus Overstimulation

Your sensory system might simultaneously seek certain types of input while being easily overwhelmed by others. **You might crave intense music or movement (ADHD stimulation seeking) while being overwhelmed by unexpected sounds or touch (autism sensory sensitivity).**

This can create seemingly contradictory behaviors – you might seek out busy, stimulating environments for the energy they provide, then need to leave suddenly when the stimulation becomes overwhelming. **Or you might create elaborate sensory environments at home that provide exactly the right amount and type of stimulation.**

Understanding this dynamic helps you recognize that you're not being inconsistent or difficult – **you're managing complex sensory needs that require more nuanced solutions than simple "more" or "less" stimulation.**

Social Connection Versus Social Exhaustion

Many people with AuDHD experience both genuine desire for social connection and real exhaustion from social interaction. **Your ADHD brain might crave the stimulation and engagement that comes from social interaction, while your autistic brain finds the unpredictability and communication demands exhausting.**

This can lead to patterns where you seek out social situations for the energy and stimulation they provide, then feel completely drained afterward and need extended recovery time. **You might appear very social and outgoing during gatherings, then disappear completely for days or weeks afterward.**

Neither the social seeking nor the social exhaustion is wrong – they're both legitimate responses from different aspects of your neurological system. Understanding this can help you plan for social activities more realistically and communicate your needs to others more effectively.

Deep Focus Versus Scattered Attention

Your attention system might be capable of incredibly deep focus on preferred topics while struggling with sustained attention on less engaging tasks. **This creates what many people experience as inconsistent or unpredictable attention capabilities.**

You might spend eight hours completely absorbed in researching a topic that interests you, then struggle to focus for five minutes on administrative tasks. **This isn't laziness or lack of discipline – it's your brain's attention system working optimally under certain conditions and suboptimally under others.**

Understanding this pattern allows you to structure tasks and environments in ways that work with your attention patterns rather than fighting against them. This might involve batching similar tasks, creating accountability systems, or finding ways to make necessary but boring tasks more engaging.

Executive Function in AuDHD (Different from ADHD Alone)

Executive function – the brain's management system for planning, organizing, prioritizing, and completing tasks – works differently in AuDHD brains than in either autism or ADHD alone. **Understanding these differences is crucial for developing effective strategies rather than feeling frustrated by approaches that don't quite fit.**

The Planning Paradox

Many people with AuDHD experience what feels like contradictory planning abilities. You might be capable of incredibly detailed, systematic planning for projects that interest you, while struggling to plan basic daily activities. **This reflects the interaction between autism's systematic thinking and ADHD's interest-based attention.**

Your brain might excel at complex project management when the task engages both your special interests and provides sufficient stimulation, but struggle with routine planning that feels boring or overwhelming. **This isn't inconsistent capability – it's consistent patterns based on different types of cognitive engagement.**

Understanding this helps you recognize that you do have strong planning abilities – they just require the right conditions to function optimally. **You can work with this pattern by finding ways to make routine planning more engaging or by creating systems that accommodate your brain's natural planning style.**

Organization Systems That Flex

Traditional organization systems often fail for AuDHD brains because they're designed to be either completely systematic (which might not provide enough stimulation) or completely flexible (which might not provide enough structure). **Your brain likely needs organization systems that provide structure while allowing for modification and personalization.**

You might find that you create elaborate organizational systems that work brilliantly for a while, then gradually abandon them as they become too rigid or boring. **This isn't failure – it's your brain** signaling that the system needs to evolve to continue meeting your changing needs.

Effective AuDHD organization systems build in flexibility and regular review periods. They provide enough structure to reduce decision fatigue while allowing enough customization to maintain interest and accommodate changing circumstances.

Task Completion Patterns

Task completion in AuDHD brains often follows patterns that don't match traditional productivity advice. **You might work intensively on projects in bursts, complete tasks in unusual orders, or need to finish things all at once rather than gradually.**

These patterns often reflect the interaction between autism's need for completion and closure with ADHD's attention patterns. **You might find it difficult to stop working on something once you've started (autism) while also needing that work to be sufficiently engaging to maintain attention (ADHD).**

Understanding your natural task completion patterns allows you to plan projects in ways that work with your brain's rhythm rather than fighting against it. This might mean scheduling intensive work periods followed by recovery time, or breaking large projects into completion-sized chunks that satisfy your brain's need for closure.

Sensory Experiences: Seeker AND Avoider

The sensory experience of AuDHD often involves simultaneous seeking and avoiding behaviors that can feel confusing to yourself and others. **Your sensory system might actively seek certain types of input while being highly sensitive to others, creating what appears to be inconsistent responses.**

The Sensory Paradox

You might find yourself craving intense sensory experiences in some areas while being easily overwhelmed by seemingly minor sensations in others. **This might mean seeking out loud music while being overwhelmed by background noise, or loving certain textures while being unable to tolerate others.**

This isn't inconsistency – it's your brain having specific sensory preferences and requirements that are more complex than simple seeking or avoiding patterns. Your sensory system might need exactly the right type of input at the right intensity for optimal functioning.

Understanding this paradox helps explain why sensory recommendations designed for autism-only or ADHD-only individuals might not work for you. **You need strategies that account for both sensory seeking and sensory sensitivity simultaneously.**

Environmental Optimization

Creating sensory environments that work for AuDHD brains requires careful attention to multiple factors simultaneously. **You might need background stimulation that's predictable and controllable, spaces that provide both stimulation and retreat options, or sensory tools that can be adjusted based on your current needs.**

This might involve creating different sensory zones in your living space – areas designed for high stimulation when your ADHD brain needs engagement, and areas designed for low stimulation when your autistic brain needs calm. **The key is having options available rather than trying to find one perfect sensory environment.**

You might also need portable sensory tools that help you manage different environments – headphones for controlling auditory input, fidget items for providing appropriate stimulation, or sensory break strategies for managing overwhelm.

Sensory Planning and Communication

Understanding your sensory patterns allows you to plan for different environments and communicate your needs to others more effectively. Rather than appearing randomly sensitive or difficult, you can explain that your sensory system has specific requirements that help you function optimally.

This might mean requesting certain accommodations at work, choosing social activities based on their sensory characteristics, or planning recovery time after sensory-intensive activities. **It's not about limiting your experiences – it's about participating in experiences in ways that work for your sensory system.**

Energy Management and the Burnout Cycle

Energy management in AuDHD brains involves understanding how multiple systems draw on your energy reserves and how to replenish those reserves effectively. **Traditional energy management strategies often don't account for the specific energy demands of managing both autism and ADHD traits simultaneously.**

The Multiple Energy Systems

Your brain uses energy for multiple purposes simultaneously: masking autism traits, managing ADHD symptoms, processing sensory information, maintaining social connections, and completing daily tasks. Each of these systems has energy requirements, and they can compete for limited resources.

Understanding that you're managing multiple energy systems simultaneously helps explain why you might feel exhausted after activities that seem simple to others. **You're not less capable – you're managing more complex energy requirements.**

This also explains why energy management strategies designed for neurotypical individuals often don't work for AuDHD brains. **You need approaches that account for your specific energy requirements and replenishment needs.**

Recognizing Energy Depletion

Energy depletion in AuDHD brains often has specific warning signs that are different from typical tiredness. **You might experience increased sensory sensitivity, decreased ability to mask or** socialize, difficulty with routine tasks that are usually manageable, or increased emotional reactivity.

Learning to recognize these early warning signs allows you to take action before reaching complete burnout. **This might mean reducing commitments, increasing self-care activities, or modifying your environment to reduce energy demands.**

Energy depletion is not a character flaw or sign of weakness – it's important information about your brain's resource management that deserves attention and respect.

Sustainable Energy Practices

Sustainable energy management for AuDHD brains involves both reducing unnecessary energy expenditure and actively replenishing energy reserves. This might mean identifying which masking behaviors are essential versus habitual, creating more sensory-friendly environments, or establishing routines that support rather than drain your energy.

Energy replenishment often requires activities that specifically address AuDHD needs – this might mean engaging with special interests, spending time in optimal sensory environments, having social connection that doesn't require masking, or physical activities that provide appropriate stimulation without overwhelming your system.

The goal isn't to eliminate all energy expenditure – it's to make conscious choices about where you spend your energy and ensure you have effective ways to replenish what you use.

Breaking the Burnout Cycle

Many people with unrecognized AuDHD develop patterns of chronic burnout – periods of high functioning followed by complete exhaustion, followed by gradual recovery and then repetition of the cycle. **Understanding your AuDHD traits can help break this cycle by creating more sustainable approaches to energy management.**

This involves learning to recognize your energy patterns, planning for energy-intensive activities, and building regular replenishment into your routine rather than waiting for crisis points. **It also involves developing self-advocacy skills to communicate your energy needs to others and modify environments to be more sustainable.**

Breaking the burnout cycle doesn't happen overnight, but it's possible with consistent attention to your actual energy requirements rather than trying to meet neurotypical energy expectations.

Personal Brain Mapping Exercise

Understanding your unique AuDHD brain requires systematic exploration of your own patterns and preferences. **This exercise helps you develop a personalized understanding of how your brain works most effectively.**

Attention Pattern Mapping

Track your attention patterns across different types of activities, environments, and times of day. **Notice when your focus feels effortless versus when it requires significant energy, what types of tasks capture your attention easily, and how environmental factors affect your ability to concentrate.**

Pay attention to the difference between chosen focus (activities you select) and required focus (activities you must do), and how your attention patterns change based on your interest level, energy status, and environmental conditions.

This information helps you understand your attention as a complex system rather than a simple strength or weakness, allowing you to structure tasks and environments to work with your natural patterns.

Sensory Preference Assessment

Systematically explore your sensory preferences across different systems – visual, auditory, tactile, vestibular, proprioceptive, and interoceptive. **Notice which types of sensory input feel energizing versus draining, which environments support your optimal functioning, and how your sensory needs change throughout the day.**

Document both sensory seeking and sensory avoiding patterns, paying attention to how these might be related. **You might discover that you seek certain types of input to help manage sensitivity to other types, or that your sensory needs are highly dependent on your energy level and stress status.**

This assessment helps you create sensory environments and strategies that support rather than drain your energy, and communicate your sensory needs to others more effectively.

Energy Pattern Recognition

Track your energy levels and patterns over time, paying attention to what activities drain versus replenish your energy, how different environments affect your energy status, and what early warning signs indicate energy depletion.

Notice the difference between physical tiredness and the specific type of exhaustion that comes from managing AuDHD traits. This might involve different types of recovery and replenishment strategies.

Understanding your energy patterns allows you to plan activities more sustainably, advocate for accommodations that support your energy management, and develop personalized strategies for maintaining optimal functioning.

Contradiction Management Strategies

Living successfully with AuDHD requires developing strategies for managing the internal contradictions that come with having both autism and ADHD traits. **These strategies help you honor both sets of needs rather than constantly choosing one over the other.**

Creating Flexible Structure

Develop organizational and planning systems that provide structure while allowing for modification and spontaneity. **This might mean creating routines that have built-in flexibility points, or establishing systems that can be easily modified without completely abandoning them.**

The goal is providing enough predictability to satisfy your autism brain while maintaining enough flexibility to accommodate your ADHD brain's need for novelty and change.

Gradual Accommodation

When you recognize competing needs, practice gradual accommodation strategies that allow you to address both needs over time rather than immediately choosing one over the other. **This might mean gradually increasing social activities when you've been isolated, or gradually reducing commitments when you're feeling overwhelmed.**

These strategies help you avoid the all-or-nothing patterns that often develop when trying to manage competing neurological needs.

Environmental Zoning

Create different environments or spaces that serve different aspects of your neurological needs. **This might mean having both high-stimulation and low-stimulation areas in your home, or developing different strategies for different types of social situations.**

The key is having options available rather than trying to find one perfect solution that addresses all your needs simultaneously.

Communication Frameworks

Develop language for explaining your contradictory needs to others in ways that help them understand rather than dismiss your requirements. **This might involve explaining that you need both social connection and alone time, or that you need both structure and flexibility in work environments.**

Having clear language for your needs helps others understand that you're not being difficult or inconsistent – you're managing complex neurological requirements that deserve respect and accommodation.

These discoveries guide us toward understanding how your authentic self can emerge when you stop trying to fit neurotypical expectations and start working with your actual neurological patterns. **The goal isn't to eliminate the contradictions of AuDHD – it's to develop strategies that honor all aspects of your unique neurological profile.**

Chapter 4: The Unmasking Journey

Finding Your Authentic Self Safely

Have you ever felt like you're playing a character in your own life? You know the feeling – carefully monitoring your words, adjusting your body language, calculating how much enthusiasm to show for your interests, or forcing yourself to make small talk when you'd rather be silent. For people with AuDHD, this performance often becomes so automatic that you might not even realize you're doing it anymore.

This performance has a name: masking. And while it serves important survival functions, it also comes with hidden costs that many people don't recognize until they begin the process of unmasking – gradually revealing and accepting their authentic selves.

Unmasking isn't about suddenly throwing caution to the wind or abandoning all social awareness. It's about making conscious choices about when, where, and how to be authentic, rather than automatically defaulting to performance mode in every situation.

For many people discovering their AuDHD, the idea of unmasking feels both thrilling and terrifying. Thrilling because it promises relief from the exhaustion of constant performance. Terrifying because the mask has provided protection, acceptance, and success in a world that often doesn't understand neurodivergent ways of being.

The key to successful unmasking is understanding that it's not an all-or-nothing process. It's a gradual, strategic journey of finding safe spaces and relationships where you can be increasingly authentic while maintaining appropriate boundaries in situations where masking still serves your goals and wellbeing.

What Masking Really Is and Its Cost

Masking is the conscious or unconscious suppression of your natural responses and behaviors in order to appear more neurotypical. **For people with AuDHD, masking often involves managing two different sets of traits simultaneously** – suppressing autistic behaviors while also controlling ADHD impulses, creating a complex performance that requires enormous mental energy.

The Complexity of AuDHD Masking

When you have both autism and ADHD, masking becomes particularly sophisticated because you're not just hiding one set of traits – you're managing multiple, sometimes contradictory performances. You might suppress your natural stimming behaviors (autism masking) while also forcing yourself to sit still and appear focused (ADHD masking), all while monitoring social cues and maintaining appropriate conversation flow.

This creates what many people describe as feeling like they're running multiple programs simultaneously – one program monitoring social expectations, another managing sensory input, another controlling physical impulses, and yet another maintaining the appearance of neurotypical attention and engagement.

A working professional might spend their day suppressing their need to move and fidget, forcing eye contact during meetings, pretending to follow conversations that jump between topics without clear transitions, and showing appropriate levels of enthusiasm for projects that don't genuinely interest them. By evening, they feel completely depleted, having used enormous amounts of mental energy to maintain these performances throughout the day.

The Hidden Energy Drain

One of the most significant costs of masking is the energy expenditure that others rarely see or understand. **Masking requires constant cognitive monitoring and control, which uses the same mental resources needed for other cognitive tasks.** This means you're essentially running a background program at all times that consumes processing power needed for other activities.

This energy drain helps explain why you might feel exhausted after social situations that others find energizing, why you need more recovery time after work or social events, or why you sometimes feel completely depleted even when you haven't done anything that seems particularly demanding.

The energy cost of masking also compounds over time. What might be manageable for a few hours becomes unsustainable when maintained for days, weeks, or years. This is why many people experience burnout that seems disproportionate to their external circumstances – they've been managing invisible energy demands that others don't recognize.

Loss of Authentic Connection

Perhaps the most painful cost of extensive masking is the impact on relationships and self-connection. **When you're constantly performing neurotypical behavior, others are connecting with your mask rather than your authentic self.** This can create a profound sense of loneliness, even in close relationships.

You might find yourself wondering if people would still like you if they knew how you really think, process information, or experience the world. **This uncertainty can prevent the deep intimacy that comes from being known and accepted for who you truly are.**

Masking can also disconnect you from your own authentic preferences, needs, and reactions. After years of automatically suppressing natural responses, you might genuinely lose touch with what you actually enjoy, need, or want in different situations.

Physical and Emotional Costs

The stress of constant masking can manifest in physical symptoms – headaches, muscle tension, digestive issues, or chronic fatigue that seems unrelated to your activity level. **Your nervous system remains in a heightened state of alertness, constantly monitoring and controlling your natural responses.**

Emotionally, extensive masking can contribute to anxiety, depression, and a sense of disconnection from yourself and others. You might experience what feels like imposter syndrome – a sense that you're fraudulent or that your successes aren't "real" because they were achieved while masking.

Some people describe feeling like they don't know who they really are anymore after years of automatic masking in most situations. This identity confusion is a natural result of spending so much energy managing your external presentation that you lose touch with your internal experience.

Why Unmasking Isn't Instant or Complete

Many people approach unmasking with the expectation that they can simply decide to stop masking and immediately begin expressing their authentic selves in all situations. **In reality, unmasking is a gradual process that requires careful consideration, practice, and ongoing adjustment.**

The Protective Function of Masking

Before beginning to unmask, it's important to recognize that your masking behaviors developed for good reasons. **They helped you navigate social situations, succeed in educational and professional environments, and avoid negative consequences in a world that often doesn't accommodate neurodivergent differences.**

Acknowledging that masking served protective functions doesn't mean you need to continue all masking behaviors indefinitely. **But it does mean that unmasking needs to happen thoughtfully, with consideration for the functions that masking served and alternative ways to meet those needs.**

You might have developed masking strategies that helped you make friends, succeed at work, or maintain family relationships. Before abandoning these strategies entirely, consider what authentic alternatives might serve similar functions while requiring less energy and allowing for more genuine connection.

Habitual and Unconscious Patterns

Many masking behaviors become so automatic that you perform them without conscious awareness. **After years or decades of suppressing natural responses, the suppression itself becomes natural.** This means that unmasking often requires first becoming aware of masking behaviors you didn't realize you were performing.

You might discover that you automatically adjust your posture in certain settings, modify your speech patterns around different groups of people, or suppress stimming behaviors so consistently that you've forgotten you have the urge to stim. **Becoming conscious of these patterns is the first step in deciding which ones to modify.**

Some masking behaviors might feel so ingrained that changing them requires significant practice and patience with yourself. **This isn't failure or resistance – it's the natural result of neural pathways that have been reinforced for years.**

Environmental and Social Constraints

Not all environments are safe for complete authenticity, and strategic masking remains important in certain situations. **Unmasking successfully requires developing judgment about when, where, and with whom it's safe and appropriate to be fully authentic.**

Professional environments might require certain levels of masking for practical reasons, even as you work toward greater authenticity. Family relationships might need gradual adjustment as you help others understand your authentic self. **The goal isn't to unmask everywhere immediately, but to make conscious choices about your level of authenticity in different situations.**

This selective approach to unmasking allows you to begin experiencing the relief and connection that comes from authenticity while maintaining appropriate boundaries and protection in situations where full authenticity might not be safe or practical.

Identity Integration Process

Unmasking also involves integrating previously suppressed aspects of yourself with the parts of your identity that you've been comfortable expressing. **This integration takes time and often involves some confusion or uncertainty as you rediscover authentic preferences and responses.**

You might find that some aspects of your "authentic self" feel uncomfortable or unfamiliar after years of suppression. **This doesn't mean these aspects aren't genuinely you – it means you need time to become reacquainted with parts of yourself that you've kept hidden.**

The process might involve some trial and error as you experiment with different levels of authenticity in various situations and notice how these experiments affect your energy, relationships, and overall wellbeing.

Strategic Unmasking: When, Where, and With Whom

Successful unmasking involves developing strategic awareness about the contexts and relationships where increased authenticity is most likely to be safe, beneficial, and sustainable. **This approach allows you to experience the benefits of authenticity while maintaining necessary protections.**

Creating Safe Spaces

Begin your unmasking journey by identifying or creating spaces where you can be increasingly authentic with minimal risk of negative consequences. **These might be private spaces in your home, relationships with understanding friends or family members, or communities specifically designed to support neurodivergent individuals.**

Safe spaces for unmasking share certain characteristics: they're predictable, accepting of neurodivergent traits, free from judgment or pressure to perform, and populated by people who value authenticity over conformity. **These spaces allow you to practice being authentic without the stress of managing others' reactions or potential negative consequences.**

You might start by creating physical safe spaces – areas in your home where you can stim freely, engage with special interests without time limits, or simply exist without monitoring your behavior. **These spaces become laboratories for rediscovering your authentic responses and preferences.**

Online communities can also provide safe spaces for initial unmasking, allowing you to express thoughts and experiences that you might not feel comfortable sharing in face-to-face interactions initially.

Relationship Assessment

Evaluate your current relationships for their capacity to support your authentic self. **Some relationships might already be more accepting of neurodivergent traits than you realized, while others might require gradual education and boundary-setting to become safer for authenticity.**

Consider which people in your life have demonstrated acceptance of differences, curiosity about your experiences, and flexibility in their expectations. **These individuals might be good candidates for early unmasking experiments.**

You might also notice that some relationships have been sustained primarily through masking and might not survive increased authenticity. **While this can be painful to recognize, it also opens space for relationships based on genuine connection rather than performance.**

The goal isn't to test every relationship simultaneously, but to begin with the relationships that feel safest and most likely to respond positively to increased authenticity.

Professional Considerations

Workplace unmasking requires particularly careful consideration because professional environments often have explicit and implicit expectations for behavior and communication style. **However, this**

doesn't mean professional authenticity is impossible – it means it needs to be approached strategically.

Start by identifying which aspects of professional masking are truly necessary versus habitual. You might discover that some masking behaviors aren't actually required by your work environment but have become automatic responses to professional settings.

Consider gradually introducing small authentic elements – perhaps stimming tools that aren't disruptive, more direct communication about your needs, or requests for accommodations that support your optimal functioning.

Some professional environments might be more receptive to neurodivergent authenticity than others. **Companies with diversity and inclusion initiatives, creative industries, or workplaces that already employ neurodivergent individuals might be more open to accommodating authentic neurodivergent expression.**

Family Dynamics

Family unmasking often involves complex dynamics because family members have known you in masked form for years or decades and might resist changes in your self-expression. **Family members might interpret your unmasking as rejection of them or as a phase you're going through rather than as authentic self-expression.**

Approach family unmasking gradually, with clear communication about what's changing and why. **Help family members understand that unmasking isn't about rejecting them or your shared history, but about reducing the energy drain of constant performance so you can be more present and genuine in relationships.**

Some family members might be surprisingly supportive once they understand that your masking was causing stress and exhaustion. Others might need time to adjust to your more authentic expressions of neurodivergent traits.

Set clear boundaries about which comments and feedback are helpful versus harmful as you navigate this process with family members.

The Vulnerability of Authenticity

Choosing authenticity over masking involves accepting increased vulnerability – the possibility that others might not understand, accept, or appreciate your genuine self. **This vulnerability is both the risk and the reward of unmasking.**

Fear of Rejection

One of the most significant barriers to unmasking is the fear that others will reject your authentic self. **This fear is often based on real experiences of negative reactions to neurodivergent traits, making it a rational concern rather than irrational anxiety.**

You might have learned early in life that certain aspects of your authentic self – your intense interests, sensory needs, communication style, or emotional expressions – received negative feedback from others. **These experiences understandably create hesitation about revealing these aspects of yourself again.**

However, continuing to mask all authentic traits guarantees that you'll never experience acceptance of your genuine self. The vulnerability of authenticity at least creates the possibility of genuine connection and understanding.

Consider that rejection of your authentic self, while painful, provides important information about which relationships and environments truly support your wellbeing versus those that require you to maintain exhausting performances.

Imposter Syndrome and Self-Doubt

As you begin unmasking, you might experience increased self-doubt about whether your authentic expressions are "too much" or inappropriate. **This doubt often reflects internalized messages** about neurodivergent traits rather than accurate feedback about your actual impact on others.

You might catch yourself second-guessing authentic responses, wondering if you're being "too autistic" or "too ADHD" in various situations. **These concerns often reflect years of conditioning to suppress natural responses rather than genuine problems with your authentic expression.**

Learning to trust your authentic instincts after years of suppressing them takes practice and patience with yourself. Some experimentation and adjustment is natural as you recalibrate your self-expression.

Managing Others' Reactions

Not everyone will respond positively to your increased authenticity, and learning to manage others' reactions without immediately reverting to masking is an important skill in the unmasking process. **Some people might express surprise, confusion, or even criticism as you begin expressing previously suppressed traits.**

Remember that others' reactions often reflect their own comfort levels and understanding rather than accurate assessments of your appropriateness or value. People who have known you only in masked form might need time to adjust to your more authentic expression.

Develop strategies for managing negative reactions that don't involve immediately abandoning authenticity. **This might mean having prepared responses to common criticisms, seeking support from understanding individuals, or removing yourself from situations where authenticity isn't safe or valued.**

The Courage to Continue

Authenticity requires ongoing courage because it involves repeatedly choosing vulnerability over the safety of performance. **This courage doesn't eliminate fear or uncertainty – it means continuing to pursue authentic expression despite these natural concerns.**

Each positive experience with authenticity builds confidence for future authentic expressions. Start with small experiments in safe spaces and gradually expand your comfort zone as you develop evidence that authenticity can lead to positive outcomes.

Remember that the goal isn't universal acceptance of your authentic self – it's finding the relationships and environments where authenticity is valued and rewarded so you can spend less energy on performance and more energy on genuine connection and contribution.

Dealing with Rejection of Your True Self

Despite careful strategic unmasking, you will likely encounter some negative reactions to your authentic self. **Learning to handle these reactions without abandoning authenticity is crucial for sustaining the unmasking process.**

Understanding Different Types of Rejection

Not all negative reactions to authenticity represent the same type of rejection. **Some reactions reflect lack of understanding that can be addressed through education and communication. Others reflect fundamental incompatibility with your authentic self.**

Reactions based on misunderstanding might include surprise at your stimming behaviors, confusion about your communication style, or concern about changes in your social participation. **These reactions often improve with patient explanation and time for adjustment.**

Reactions based on judgment or intolerance might include criticism of your authentic traits as inappropriate, demands that you suppress natural behaviors, or dismissal of your neurodivergent needs. **These reactions indicate relationships or environments that may not be compatible with your authentic wellbeing.**

Learning to distinguish between these types of reactions helps you respond appropriately – providing education where there's openness to learning and setting boundaries where there's resistance to acceptance.

Protecting Your Self-Worth

When others respond negatively to your authentic self, it's natural to question whether there's something wrong with your authentic expression. **Developing strong internal validation becomes crucial for maintaining self-worth during the unmasking process.**

Remember that your worth isn't determined by others' acceptance of your neurodivergent traits. Your authentic self deserves respect and accommodation, not because others approve, but because you're a valuable person with legitimate needs and perspectives.

Negative reactions often say more about others' limitations than about problems with your authenticity. **Some people lack the flexibility, understanding, or emotional capacity to appreciate neurodivergent ways of being – this reflects their constraints, not your deficiencies.**

Build relationships and communities that affirm your authentic worth so you have sources of validation when you encounter rejection or misunderstanding.

Boundary Setting with Non-Accepting Individuals

When people consistently respond negatively to your authentic self despite clear communication and reasonable accommodation attempts, **boundary setting becomes necessary for protecting your wellbeing and continued authenticity.**

These boundaries might involve limiting the topics you discuss with certain individuals, reducing the time spent in unsupportive environments, or ending relationships that consistently require excessive masking to maintain.

Setting boundaries isn't about punishing others for their limitations – it's about protecting your energy and mental health so you can continue pursuing authenticity in relationships and environments that are more supportive.

Some relationships might require ongoing boundaries about which aspects of your authentic self you share. **This isn't failure at unmasking – it's wise stewardship of your energy and emotional resources.**

Finding Your Community

One of the most powerful antidotes to rejection is finding community with others who understand and appreciate your authentic self. **Neurodivergent communities, both online and in-person, can provide the understanding and validation that support continued authenticity.**

These communities offer the experience of being understood without extensive explanation, accepted without performance, and valued for contributions that arise from your neurodivergent perspectives and abilities.

You don't need universal acceptance to live authentically – you need enough acceptance to sustain your wellbeing and sense of belonging. Focus on cultivating relationships and communities that genuinely appreciate your authentic contributions.

Masking Inventory: What Am I Still Performing?

Understanding which masking behaviors you currently engage in is the first step toward making conscious choices about authenticity. **This inventory helps you identify both obvious and subtle masking patterns that might be consuming your energy.**

Social Masking Assessment

Examine your social behaviors across different contexts and relationships. **Notice which social responses feel automatic versus authentic, what aspects of your personality you modify in different social situations, and which social activities drain versus energize you.**

Consider your conversation patterns – do you find yourself showing interest in topics that don't genuinely engage you? Do you suppress your own interests to avoid seeming "too intense" or "weird"? Do you mirror others' energy levels rather than expressing your natural responses?

Pay attention to your body language and physical presentation in social situations. Are you suppressing natural movement patterns, forcing eye contact that feels uncomfortable, or maintaining facial expressions that don't match your internal experience?

Notice your social participation patterns – are you forcing yourself to attend social events that consistently drain your energy? Are you saying yes to social commitments out of obligation rather than genuine interest?

Emotional Masking Patterns

Examine how you express emotions in different contexts. **Many people with AuDHD learn to suppress or modify emotional expressions to appear more neurotypical, which can disconnect them from their authentic emotional experience.**

Consider which emotions you feel comfortable expressing authentically versus which ones you feel pressure to modify or hide. You might find that you suppress excitement about special interests, hide overwhelm or frustration, or force positive emotions in situations where you're struggling.

Notice whether your emotional expressions feel genuine or performed in different relationships and environments. Are there situations where you feel safe to express the full range of your emotional experience?

Pay attention to emotional recovery patterns – do you need more time alone after emotional conversations or situations than others seem to need? This might indicate that emotional masking is consuming additional energy.

Professional Masking Review

Workplace masking often involves complex layers of behavioral modification to meet professional expectations. **Examine which aspects of your professional presentation feel authentic versus performed.**

Consider your communication patterns at work – are you modifying your natural directness, suppressing questions about unclear instructions, or forcing enthusiasm for projects that don't genuinely interest you?

Notice your physical behavior in professional settings – are you suppressing stimming behaviors, forcing yourself to sit still in meetings, or maintaining workspace organization that doesn't match your natural patterns?

Examine your professional social participation – are you attending networking events or team social activities that consistently drain your energy? Are you engaging in small talk that feels meaningless or forced?

Sensory Masking Identification

Many people with AuDHD suppress natural responses to sensory input, which can create additional stress and energy drain. **Notice which sensory accommodations you avoid making because they might appear "different" or "demanding."**

Consider your sensory environment choices – are you tolerating lighting, sound, or temperature conditions that genuinely bother you to avoid seeming "difficult"? Are you suppressing visible reactions to sensory input that feels overwhelming?

Pay attention to sensory-seeking behaviors you might be suppressing – do you want to move, touch certain textures, or seek specific types of sensory input but hold back because it might seem inappropriate?

Notice your sensory recovery needs – do you require more sensory downtime than you're currently allowing yourself? This might indicate that you're masking sensory sensitivities during regular activities.

Unmasking Safety Assessment Tool

Before beginning to unmask in any situation, **assess the safety and appropriateness of increased authenticity in that specific context.** This tool helps you make strategic decisions about when and where to unmask.

Environmental Safety Factors

Evaluate the physical and social environment for characteristics that support versus hinder authentic expression. **Safe environments typically have predictable expectations, tolerance for differences, and minimal consequences for neurodivergent behaviors.**

Consider the power dynamics in the environment – are you in a position where authenticity might affect your job security, housing, or other essential needs? **High-stakes environments might require more cautious approaches to unmasking.**

Assess the sensory characteristics of the environment – is it a space where your sensory needs can be accommodated, or where sensory overwhelm might make authenticity more difficult to manage?

Notice whether the environment has explicit or implicit diversity and inclusion values that might support neurodivergent expression, or whether conformity and traditional behavior are strongly emphasized.

Relationship Safety Evaluation

Examine specific relationships for their capacity to handle increased authenticity. **Safe relationships typically demonstrate curiosity about your experiences, flexibility in their expectations, and respect for your needs and boundaries.**

Consider the history of the relationship – have these individuals demonstrated acceptance of differences in the past? Have they responded positively when you've shared vulnerable information or expressed needs?

Evaluate the reciprocity in the relationship – is there mutual sharing of authentic experiences, or does the relationship require you to be the only one accommodating and performing?

Notice whether the relationship involves people who have their own neurodivergent traits or understanding of neurodiversity, which might create natural acceptance of your authentic expression.

Consequence Assessment

Realistically evaluate the potential positive and negative consequences of increased authenticity in specific situations. **This isn't about avoiding all risk, but about making informed decisions about which risks are worth taking.**

Consider the best-case scenario of authenticity – what positive outcomes might result from more genuine expression in this situation? This might include reduced energy drain, deeper connection, or better accommodation of your needs.

Evaluate the worst-case scenario honestly – what negative consequences are realistically possible if authenticity is not well-received? Consider whether these consequences are temporary and manageable or severe and long-lasting.

Assess your current capacity to handle both positive and negative outcomes – do you have sufficient emotional and practical support to manage various responses to your authenticity?

Progressive Unmasking Plan Template

Successful unmasking typically happens gradually rather than all at once. This template provides a structure for systematically increasing authenticity while building confidence and support systems.

Phase 1: Safe Space Authenticity

Begin unmasking in your safest environments and relationships. **This might involve being authentic in private spaces, with your most understanding friends, or in online communities designed for neurodivergent individuals.**

Start with low-risk authentic expressions – perhaps stimming freely at home, sharing interests without editing your enthusiasm, or communicating your needs directly in safe relationships.

Use this phase to reconnect with suppressed aspects of your authentic self and build confidence in your ability to express these aspects appropriately.

Document your experiences during this phase – what feels energizing versus draining about increased authenticity? What authentic expressions feel most natural and comfortable?

Phase 2: Selective Context Expansion

Gradually expand authenticity to additional contexts that feel moderately safe. **This might involve being more authentic with family members who have shown understanding, requesting specific accommodations at work, or joining neurodivergent community groups.**

Choose specific authentic behaviors to practice in these expanded contexts – perhaps asking for sensory accommodations, expressing your interests more freely, or setting boundaries about your social energy.

Continue to maintain appropriate masking in high-risk situations while building your capacity and confidence for authenticity in increasingly diverse contexts.

Gather feedback about your authentic expressions in these expanded contexts and adjust your approach based on what you learn about others' receptivity and your own comfort levels.

Phase 3: Strategic Integration

Develop a sustainable long-term approach that integrates authenticity into most areas of your life while maintaining strategic masking where necessary. **This phase involves fine-tuning your judgment about when, where, and how to be authentic.**

Create clear boundaries about which environments and relationships support authenticity versus those where strategic masking remains important for practical reasons.

Develop skills for handling negative reactions to authenticity without immediately reverting to complete masking. This might involve prepared responses, support systems, or strategies for managing difficult situations.

Build ongoing support systems that sustain your authenticity over time – this might include therapy, neurodivergent community involvement, or accountability partnerships with understanding individuals.

Boundary-Setting Scripts

Clear communication about your needs and limits is essential for sustaining authenticity while maintaining healthy relationships. These scripts provide language for common boundary-setting situations during the unmasking process.

Sensory Boundary Scripts

"I have specific sensory needs that help me function at my best. I'd like to discuss some accommodations that would help me participate more effectively."

"I need to take breaks from sensory-intensive environments to prevent overwhelm. This isn't personal – it's how my nervous system works best."

"I'd like to explain why I might need to use headphones, fidget tools, or take sensory breaks. These accommodations help me stay focused and engaged."

Communication Boundary Scripts

"I communicate most effectively when I can be direct about my needs and concerns. This isn't intended to be rude – it's actually my way of being respectful and clear."

"I process information differently and might need extra time to respond to complex questions or decisions. This helps me give you thoughtful, accurate responses."

"I'd like to share some information about how I communicate naturally so we can avoid misunderstandings and work together more effectively."

Social Energy Boundary Scripts

"I have limited social energy and need to be strategic about how I use it. This means I might need to decline some social invitations to preserve energy for activities that are most important."

"I need quiet time after social activities to recharge. This isn't about not enjoying the time together – it's about managing my energy so I can continue to show up for important relationships."

"I'd like to find ways to connect that work well for both of us. This might mean shorter visits, different types of activities, or advance planning that helps me prepare."

Workplace Authenticity Scripts

"I work most effectively when I can use strategies that match how my brain functions. I'd like to discuss some accommodations that would help me perform at my best."

"I have some neurological differences that affect how I process information and interact with others. Understanding these differences can help us work together more effectively."

"I'm committed to contributing effectively to our team. There are some adjustments to my work environment or responsibilities that would help me do my best work."

Armed with this understanding of the unmasking process, you can begin the parallel work of reconstructing your identity – discovering who you are when you're not constantly performing neurotypical behaviors. This identity work is essential for sustaining authenticity and building a life that truly fits your AuDHD brain.

Chapter 5: Identity Reconstruction

Who Am I Without the Mask?

After years or decades of masking, one of the most disorienting aspects of the unmasking journey is the realization that you might not know who you really are. **When so much energy has gone into performing neurotypical behavior, your authentic preferences, reactions, and ways of being may feel unfamiliar or uncertain.**

This identity uncertainty isn't a sign of weakness or confusion – it's a natural result of having focused your attention outward on managing others' perceptions rather than inward on understanding your own authentic experience. **The person you are without the mask has always been there, but they may have been so quiet for so long that you need time to listen carefully to hear their voice again.**

Identity reconstruction after AuDHD discovery involves a process of archaeological work – carefully uncovering authentic aspects of yourself that have been buried under years of learned behaviors and social expectations. **It's not about creating a new identity from scratch, but about rediscovering and integrating parts of yourself that have always existed.**

This process can feel exciting and overwhelming simultaneously. Exciting because you're finally free to explore who you really are. Overwhelming because the possibilities might feel endless after years of constrained self-expression. **The key is approaching this exploration with curiosity and patience, understanding that identity reconstruction is an ongoing process rather than a destination.**

Some days you'll feel clear and confident about your authentic self. Other days you'll feel confused about what's genuinely you versus what you learned to perform. **Both experiences are completely** normal parts of reconstructing an identity that honors your full AuDHD experience.

Separating Authentic Self from Performed Self

One of the most challenging aspects of identity reconstruction involves distinguishing between authentic aspects of yourself and behaviors you've learned to perform to fit social expectations. **After years of automatic masking, this distinction isn't always obvious or clear-cut.**

Recognizing Performed Behaviors

Performed behaviors often have certain characteristics that distinguish them from authentic responses. **They typically require conscious effort to maintain, feel energetically draining over time, and might feel "off" or uncomfortable even when you're skilled at performing them.**

You might notice that certain aspects of your social presentation feel like you're following a script rather than responding naturally. Perhaps you've learned to show a specific level of enthusiasm for topics that don't genuinely interest you, or you automatically adjust your body language and speech patterns in professional settings.

Performed behaviors often become more obvious when you're tired, stressed, or overwhelmed – times when you don't have the energy to maintain the performance. You might find yourself reverting to more natural responses during these periods, which can provide clues about your authentic preferences and reactions.

Consider a working professional who automatically engages in small talk at the beginning of meetings, showing polite interest in colleagues' weekend activities while internally feeling impatient to begin the actual work discussion. This small talk performance might feel effortless after years of practice, but it drains energy that could be used for more meaningful interactions or work focus.

Identifying Authentic Impulses

Authentic responses tend to feel natural and energizing, even if they're different from social expectations. **They often emerge spontaneously when you feel safe and comfortable, and they typically align with your genuine interests, values, and ways of processing information.**

You might notice authentic impulses arising when you're in safe spaces or with understanding individuals – sudden excitement about topics you rarely discuss, natural body movements you usually suppress, or communication styles that feel more direct and honest than your typical social presentation.

Authentic responses often connect to your deeper values and genuine interests. They might involve intense curiosity about specific topics, strong reactions to injustice or inefficiency, or genuine care for particular causes or individuals.

Pay attention to moments when you feel most like yourself – these often occur during activities that deeply engage your interests, in relationships where you feel completely accepted, or in environments where you don't feel pressure to monitor and adjust your behavior.

The Gray Areas

Not everything falls clearly into "authentic" versus "performed" categories. Some behaviors might be partially authentic but modified for social appropriateness. Others might have started as performances but become integrated into your genuine self over time.

You might have learned communication skills that initially felt artificial but now feel like genuine tools for expressing your authentic thoughts and feelings more effectively. **Or you might have developed interests that began as attempts to connect with others but evolved into genuine passions.**

These gray areas are normal and don't need to be categorized definitively. **The goal isn't to eliminate all learned behaviors, but to make conscious choices about which behaviors serve your authentic expression and wellbeing.**

Some learned behaviors might be worth maintaining if they help you communicate your authentic self more effectively or participate in activities that genuinely matter to you, even if the behaviors themselves don't feel completely natural.

Energy as an Indicator

One of the most reliable ways to distinguish authentic from performed aspects of yourself is paying attention to energy patterns. **Authentic expression typically feels energizing or at least energy-neutral, while performance tends to be draining over time.**

Notice which activities, conversations, and self-expressions leave you feeling more energized versus depleted. **This doesn't mean authentic activities are always easy or that they never require effort, but they usually provide some form of satisfaction or fulfillment that compensates for the energy invested.**

Performed behaviors often provide external rewards – social acceptance, professional success, or conflict avoidance – but they rarely provide internal satisfaction that matches the energy investment required to maintain them.

Track your energy patterns over time to identify which aspects of your current life align with your authentic self versus those that primarily serve social expectations or external pressures.

Rediscovering Genuine Preferences and Interests

After years of focusing on socially appropriate interests and preferences, you might find yourself uncertain about what you genuinely enjoy, value, or want to pursue. **This rediscovery process involves experimentation, reflection, and gentle curiosity about your authentic responses.**

Childhood Interest Archaeology

Many authentic preferences can be traced back to childhood interests that were present before extensive social conditioning began. **These early interests often provide clues about your natural inclinations** and the types of activities that genuinely engage your AuDHD brain.

Think back to activities that completely absorbed your attention as a child – perhaps you spent hours arranging collections, creating detailed imaginary worlds, taking apart mechanical objects, or researching specific topics with intensity that others found unusual.

These childhood interests might not translate directly into current activities, but they often point toward underlying patterns of engagement that remain relevant to your authentic self. A childhood fascination with how things work might indicate ongoing interest in systems and processes, even if the specific focus has shifted.

Consider activities that you pursued despite discouragement from others or that you returned to repeatedly even when other interests came and went. **These persistent interests often indicate authentic engagement rather than social performance.**

You might also remember activities that you abandoned due to social pressure or criticism – perhaps you were told certain interests were "too intense," "weird," or inappropriate for your age or gender. **Revisiting these abandoned interests can be particularly revealing.**

Present-Moment Interest Exploration

Begin paying attention to what naturally captures your attention and curiosity in your current daily life. This might involve activities you browse online during free time, topics you find yourself researching spontaneously, or conversations that genuinely energize you.

Notice which activities make you lose track of time in a positive way – not because you're avoiding something else, but because you're genuinely engaged and absorbed. **These flow states often indicate authentic interest and engagement.**

Pay attention to your body's responses to different activities. Authentic interests often create physical sensations of excitement, engagement, or satisfaction that feel different from the more effortful engagement required for activities you pursue out of obligation.

Experiment with activities that you've been curious about but avoided because they seemed "too niche," "too intense," or "too different" from what others expect of you. Give yourself permission to explore interests that might not make sense to others but genuinely appeal to you.

Values Clarification

Understanding your authentic values – the principles and priorities that genuinely matter to you – is crucial for identity reconstruction. **Your authentic values might be different from the values you've been expressing socially or the values you think you should have.**

Consider what genuinely bothers you versus what you've been told should bother you. Your authentic values often emerge in your spontaneous reactions to unfairness, inefficiency, or situations that conflict with your deep sense of what's right or important.

Notice which causes or issues you find yourself thinking about repeatedly or researching in your free time. These ongoing concerns often reflect authentic values rather than socially expected interests.

Pay attention to decisions that feel energizing versus those that feel draining, even when both options seem equally reasonable from an external perspective. **Your authentic values often guide you toward choices that align with your genuine priorities.**

Consider the difference between values you hold intellectually and those you feel emotionally connected to. **Authentic values typically have both intellectual and emotional components that create genuine motivation for action.**

Relationship and Social Preference Discovery

Explore your authentic preferences for social connection and relationship styles. After years of accommodating others' social expectations, you might be unclear about your genuine social needs and preferences.

Notice which types of social interaction feel energizing versus draining – do you prefer small groups or one-on-one conversations? Do you enjoy social activities with structured activities or unstructured time? Do you connect better through shared interests or emotional sharing?

Pay attention to the pace of social connection that feels natural to you. Some people with AuDHD prefer intense, infrequent social connection, while others prefer lighter, more regular contact. Neither preference is better – the key is understanding your authentic pattern.

Consider your preferences for communication style – do you feel more genuine when being direct and literal, or when using more indirect and contextual communication? **Your authentic communication style might be different from what you've learned to perform in various social contexts.**

Explore your preferences for different types of relationships – are you energized by helping and supporting others, by intellectual discussion, by shared activities, or by quiet companionship? **Understanding your authentic relationship style helps you build connections that feel genuinely satisfying.**

The Imposter Syndrome of Late Diagnosis

Many people who discover their AuDHD in adulthood experience a specific type of imposter syndrome related to their neurodivergent identity. **This involves questioning whether your diagnosis is accurate, whether you're "autistic enough" or "ADHD enough," or whether you're unconsciously exaggerating traits to fit a category.**

Doubting Your Diagnosis

It's common to oscillate between feeling certain about your AuDHD identity and questioning whether you're "really" neurodivergent. **This doubt often intensifies during periods when your traits feel less obvious or when you're functioning well in masking mode.**

You might find yourself comparing your experience to stereotypical presentations of autism or ADHD and wondering if your differences are significant enough to "count" as neurodivergent. **Remember that these stereotypes often don't capture the full range of neurodivergent experiences, particularly for people with AuDHD, women, and individuals who developed sophisticated masking strategies.**

The fact that you've been able to mask effectively or succeed in neurotypical environments doesn't invalidate your neurodivergent identity. Many highly capable individuals have AuDHD traits that significantly impact their internal experience and energy levels, even when their external functioning appears typical.

Consider that your doubt might actually reflect the internalized ableism and neurodivergent stigma present in broader society, rather than accurate assessment of your neurodivergent traits.

Questioning Your Struggles

Another aspect of neurodivergent imposter syndrome involves minimizing the challenges you've experienced throughout your life. **You might find yourself thinking that your difficulties weren't "real" or significant enough to warrant a diagnosis, particularly if you've received messages throughout your life that you were being "too sensitive" or "dramatic."**

The fact that you've found ways to cope with or compensate for challenges doesn't mean the challenges weren't real or significant. Many people with unrecognized AuDHD develop remarkable resilience and coping strategies that mask the extent of their daily struggles.

Consider the energy cost of your coping strategies rather than just their effectiveness. You might have been successful at managing neurotypical expectations, but this success might have come at the cost of chronic exhaustion, anxiety, or disconnection from your authentic self.

Your struggles and differences are valid regardless of how well you've learned to manage or hide them. Effective coping doesn't erase the reality of neurodivergent differences.

Fear of Being "Too Much" or "Not Enough"

Many people with newly recognized AuDHD worry about expressing their neurodivergent traits authentically because they fear being either "too much" or "not enough" to be accepted in neurodivergent communities. **This creates a painful double bind where you feel too different for neurotypical spaces but not different enough for neurodivergent spaces.**

Remember that neurodivergent communities include people with wide ranges of traits, coping abilities, and life experiences. Your specific combination of strengths and challenges is valid within the broader spectrum of neurodivergent experience.

You don't need to prove your neurodivergence through struggling more or masking less. **Your neurodivergent identity is valid based on your internal experience and neurological differences, not on how much difficulty these differences create for you.**

The goal isn't to be "the right amount" of neurodivergent – it's to understand and honor your actual neurological differences so you can make choices that support your wellbeing and authentic expression.

Building Confidence in Your Identity

Developing confidence in your AuDHD identity involves focusing on your actual experiences rather than comparing yourself to others or trying to meet external criteria for "authenticity."

Keep a record of experiences and patterns that align with your AuDHD understanding – this might include sensory preferences, attention patterns, social energy patterns, or ways of processing information that feel different from neurotypical approaches.

Connect with other people who have similar experiences through online communities, support groups, or neurodivergent social activities. Hearing others describe experiences that match your own can help validate your understanding of yourself.

Work with neurodivergent-affirming professionals who understand the complexity of late diagnosis and can help you process the identity questions that arise during this exploration.

Remember that your neurodivergent identity doesn't need external validation to be real and meaningful. The most important validation comes from your own recognition of patterns and experiences that make sense within an AuDHD framework.

Building New Identity Narratives

Identity reconstruction involves developing new stories about who you are that integrate your AuDHD understanding with your life experiences, achievements, and relationships. **These new narratives help you understand your past experiences while creating framework for future growth and authenticity.**

Rewriting Your Personal History

Begin reinterpreting significant life events and patterns through the lens of your AuDHD understanding. This doesn't mean attributing everything to your neurodivergence, but recognizing how your neurological differences influenced your experiences and choices.

Consider academic and professional experiences that felt particularly challenging or rewarding and examine how these might relate to your AuDHD traits. Perhaps you excelled in subjects that matched your special interests but struggled with courses that required different types of information processing.

Examine relationship patterns with new understanding of your social and sensory needs. You might recognize that certain relationships felt draining because they required extensive masking, while others felt energizing because they allowed for more authentic connection.

Look at your coping strategies and survival mechanisms with appreciation for their creativity and effectiveness, rather than judgment about their necessity. **The strategies you developed to navigate neurotypical environments without understanding your differences demonstrate remarkable resourcefulness and adaptability.**

Consider how your unique perspectives and approaches, which might have been criticized as "different" or "difficult," actually represent strengths that arise from your AuDHD neurological style.

Identifying Consistent Themes and Patterns

Look for themes that have remained consistent throughout your life, even if they were expressed differently in various periods. These consistent elements often represent core aspects of your authentic self that persisted despite social pressures to conform.

You might notice consistent patterns in the types of problems you're drawn to solving, the ways you prefer to learn and process information, the environments where you feel most comfortable, or the types of relationships that feel most satisfying.

Consider your consistent values and concerns – issues that have mattered to you across different life stages, even if you expressed care for these issues in different ways or contexts.

Notice consistent sensory preferences and environmental needs that have influenced your choices throughout your life, perhaps in ways you didn't fully recognize at the time.

These consistent themes often represent authentic aspects of your identity that can be honored and expressed more fully as you continue the unmasking process.

Integration Rather Than Replacement

The goal of identity reconstruction isn't to throw away all previous aspects of your identity, but to integrate your AuDHD understanding with the full complexity of who you are. You remain a person with unique experiences, relationships, achievements, and perspectives – now with better understanding of your neurological differences.

Some aspects of your previous identity may need to be modified or understood differently, but many elements will remain valid and important. **You might discover that achievements you thought were despite your differences were actually because of the unique perspectives and approaches that come with your AuDHD brain.**

Consider how your learned skills and adaptive strategies can serve your authentic self rather than just social conformity. **Many masking skills can be repurposed as conscious tools for communication and environmental navigation when used strategically rather than automatically.**

Your identity integration includes both your challenges and your strengths, both your neurotypical adaptations and your neurodivergent authenticity. **The richest identity narratives honor this complexity rather than trying to simplify it into neat categories.**

Creating Future-Oriented Identity

As you develop understanding of your authentic self, begin creating identity narratives that point toward future growth and possibility rather than being limited by past constraints or misunderstandings.

Consider how your newfound self-understanding opens up possibilities that weren't previously available – career paths that better match your interests and abilities, relationship styles that honor your authentic needs, lifestyle choices that support rather than drain your energy.

Envision how your unique AuDHD perspectives and abilities can contribute to your communities, relationships, and chosen work in ways that feel meaningful and sustainable to you.

Your future-oriented identity should include realistic assessment of ongoing challenges while emphasizing growth, possibility, and the unique contributions you can make when operating from authenticity rather than performance.

Embracing Neurodivergent Pride

Moving beyond simply accepting your neurodivergent identity toward genuinely appreciating and celebrating your AuDHD brain represents an important milestone in identity reconstruction. This shift from tolerance to pride creates foundation for sustained authenticity and self-advocacy.

Recognizing Unique Strengths and Perspectives

Your AuDHD brain provides you with perspectives and abilities that are genuinely valuable and often rare in neurotypical environments. Beginning to recognize and appreciate these strengths is essential for developing authentic confidence.

Consider your ability to notice patterns and details that others miss, your capacity for sustained focus on topics that genuinely interest you, your creative problem-solving approaches, or your direct communication style that cuts through ambiguity to address core issues.

Many people with AuDHD demonstrate remarkable perseverance, creative thinking, strong sense of justice, loyalty in relationships, and ability to think outside conventional frameworks. These aren't consolation prizes – they're genuine strengths that benefit both you and others.

Your sensory sensitivity, while sometimes challenging, might also provide you with appreciation for beauty, awareness of environmental details, or ability to notice changes that others miss. **Your different** way of processing information might lead to insights and solutions that wouldn't occur to neurotypical thinkers.

Appreciating Your Survival and Adaptation

The fact that you've navigated neurotypical environments without understanding your neurological differences represents remarkable resilience and creativity. Rather than feeling embarrassed about years of masking, you can appreciate the sophisticated strategies you developed.

You've demonstrated the ability to learn complex social rules, adapt to various environmental demands, and find ways to contribute meaningfully to communities and relationships despite facing additional challenges that others didn't recognize.

Your experience of being different has likely contributed to enhanced empathy, creativity, and ability to think independently. These qualities benefit not only you but also the people and communities in your life.

The challenges you've faced and overcome have provided you with insights about resilience, adaptation, and the importance of authentic acceptance that can benefit others who are facing similar struggles.

Contributing to Neurodivergent Community

Your experience of late diagnosis and identity reconstruction positions you to contribute meaningfully to neurodivergent communities and broader awareness efforts. This contribution can become part of your authentic identity and purpose.

You might find fulfillment in supporting others who are going through similar discovery processes, advocating for better recognition and accommodation of neurodivergent needs, or simply modeling authentic living that shows others what's possible.

Your unique combination of lived experience, adaptive skills, and hard-won self-understanding creates a perspective that can be

valuable to others navigating similar journeys or working to create more inclusive environments.

This doesn't mean you need to become an activist or educator if those roles don't align with your interests and energy. **But recognizing that your experience has value beyond your personal growth can contribute to a sense of pride and purpose in your neurodivergent identity.**

Celebrating Neurodivergent Culture and Connection

Neurodivergent communities have their own cultures, humor, ways of connecting, and shared understandings that can be deeply satisfying to experience after years of trying to fit neurotypical expectations.

You might discover the joy of communicating with others who understand your references, share your interests with similar intensity, or process emotions and experiences in compatible ways. **These connections can feel profoundly different from relationships where you need to translate or modify your natural responses.**

Participating in neurodivergent culture – whether through online communities, local groups, or informal connections – can provide a sense of belonging and celebration that supports your ongoing authenticity.

This cultural connection doesn't mean rejecting neurotypical relationships or separating yourself from broader society. It means having access to community where your natural ways of being are not only accepted but celebrated and shared.

True Self Discovery Exercises

Systematic exploration can help you distinguish authentic aspects of yourself from learned performances. These exercises provide structure for the sometimes overwhelming process of identity reconstruction.

Values Identification Through Response Patterns

Pay attention to situations that create strong emotional responses – both positive and negative. **Your authentic values often reveal themselves through spontaneous reactions to situations that align with or conflict with what genuinely matters to you.**

Keep a record for a week of moments when you felt energized, excited, or deeply satisfied, as well as moments when you felt frustrated, angry, or disappointed. **Look for patterns in these responses that might point toward authentic values and preferences.**

Notice which news stories, social situations, or work scenarios create the strongest reactions. **Often these responses occur before conscious thought and can provide clues about your authentic priorities and concerns.**

Consider the difference between reactions you feel you should have versus those that arise naturally. **Authentic values typically create both intellectual understanding and emotional resonance.**

Interest Archaeology Project

Systematically explore interests and activities that you've been curious about but haven't pursued due to social concerns or practical constraints.

Make a list of topics you find yourself researching in your free time, activities you watch others do with curiosity, or skills you've always wondered about learning. **These often represent suppressed authentic interests.**

Set aside time each week to explore one of these interests without commitment to continued engagement. **Give yourself permission to try activities that might seem "weird," "too intense," or "impractical" by conventional standards.**

Pay attention to how these exploration activities affect your energy and mood. **Authentic interests often create excitement and engagement that feel different from activities you pursue out of obligation.**

Document which exploration activities you want to continue versus those that were interesting to try once but don't create ongoing engagement. **This information helps you distinguish between casual curiosity and authentic passion.**

Sensory and Environmental Preference Mapping

Systematically explore your preferences for different sensory environments and physical spaces to understand how your environment affects your authentic functioning.

Experiment with different lighting conditions, sound environments, levels of visual stimulation, and physical arrangements to notice which combinations support versus drain your energy.

Try working, relaxing, and socializing in different types of environments to understand how environmental factors affect your ability to be authentic and comfortable in various activities.

Notice how your environmental preferences might differ from what you've been accepting as "normal" or "appropriate." **Your authentic environmental needs might be more specific than you realized.**

Pay attention to environments where you feel most like yourself versus those where you feel the need to monitor and adjust your behavior constantly.

Communication Style Exploration

Experiment with different approaches to communication to discover your most authentic and effective styles.

Try being more direct in some conversations and notice how this affects both your energy and others' responses. **Many people with AuDHD find that their natural communication style is more direct than they've been expressing.**

Experiment with sharing your interests and enthusiasms more openly in safe relationships to notice how authentic expression affects connection quality.

Practice communicating your needs and boundaries more clearly rather than expecting others to guess or assume you'll automatically accommodate their preferences.

Pay attention to which communication approaches feel most genuine and create the connections you actually want rather than just social acceptance.

Values Clarification for AuDHD Life

Understanding your authentic values provides foundation for making decisions that align with your genuine priorities rather than external expectations. This process often reveals differences between values you've been expressing and those that genuinely motivate you.

Identifying Core Values

Examine decisions you've made that felt energizing and satisfying, even if they were difficult or unconventional. These decisions often reflect authentic values rather than socially expected choices.

Consider which causes or issues you find yourself thinking about repeatedly without external pressure or requirement. **These ongoing concerns often reflect authentic values that deserve attention and expression.**

Notice which activities and commitments you maintain even when they're challenging, versus those you abandon when external pressure decreases. **Authentic values typically provide internal motivation that sustains effort over time.**

Pay attention to situations where you've made sacrifices that felt meaningful versus those that felt resentful or obligatory. **Meaningful sacrifices often align with authentic values.**

Distinguishing Internal From External Motivation

Learn to recognize the difference between values that feel genuinely important to you versus those you think you should hold based on social expectations or family pressure.

Notice which values create emotional resonance when you think about them versus those that seem intellectually reasonable but don't create internal motivation for action.

Consider how your unique neurodivergent perspectives might lead to values that differ from conventional priorities. Your sensitivity to social justice, appreciation for authenticity, or focus on specific interests might reflect authentic values that deserve expression.

Pay attention to values that remained important to you even during periods when you received criticism or lack of understanding for holding them. **These persistent values often represent authentic priorities.**

Value-Based Decision Making

Begin making choices based on your authentic values rather than external expectations or social pressure. Start with low-stakes decisions to practice this skill before applying it to major life choices.

When facing decisions, consider which options align with your genuine values versus which seem most likely to receive approval from others. **This doesn't mean always choosing the unconventional option, but making conscious choices based on authentic priorities.**

Notice how value-aligned decisions affect your energy and satisfaction compared to decisions made primarily to meet external expectations.

Practice explaining your value-based decisions to others in ways that help them understand your reasoning without requiring their agreement or approval.

Identity Integration Timeline

Creating a realistic timeline for identity integration helps manage expectations and provides structure for the ongoing process of becoming more authentic. This process typically unfolds over months and years rather than weeks.

Phase 1: Recognition and Exploration (Months 1-6)

Focus on recognizing authentic aspects of yourself that have been suppressed or minimized. **This phase involves exploration and experimentation rather than permanent changes.**

Give yourself permission to try new activities, express previously hidden interests, and experiment with different ways of being in safe environments and relationships.

Expect confusion and uncertainty during this phase – it's normal to feel unclear about what's authentic versus performed when you're first beginning this exploration.

Document your discoveries and observations without pressure to make permanent decisions about identity or lifestyle changes.

Phase 2: Integration and Refinement (Months 6-18)

Begin integrating authentic discoveries into your daily life and relationships. **This phase involves making more sustained changes while refining your understanding of your authentic self.**

Start making life choices based on your growing self-understanding – this might involve changing social commitments, work responsibilities, or environmental arrangements.

Develop skills for maintaining authenticity in challenging environments while building support systems that reinforce your genuine self-expression.

Expect ongoing refinement and adjustment as you learn more about sustainable ways to honor your authentic self while meeting practical life requirements.

Phase 3: Authentic Living and Advocacy (18+ Months)

Establish sustainable patterns of authentic living that honor your AuDHD identity while maintaining important relationships and responsibilities. **This phase involves confidence in your authentic self and ability to advocate for your needs.**

Begin contributing to others' understanding of neurodivergence through your example of authentic living and willingness to educate others about AuDHD experiences.

Develop long-term goals and life plans that align with your authentic values and neurological needs rather than trying to fit neurotypical expectations.

Continue growing and adapting your authentic expression while maintaining the foundation of self-understanding and self-acceptance you've built.

Affirmation Development Guide

Creating personalized affirmations that reflect your authentic AuDHD identity can support ongoing self-acceptance and confidence. Effective affirmations address common areas of self-doubt while reinforcing positive aspects of your neurodivergent experience.

Core Identity Affirmations

"My AuDHD brain processes information in valuable and unique ways that contribute to my relationships and communities."

"I deserve acceptance and accommodation for my neurological differences, not because I've earned it, but because I'm a valuable person with legitimate needs."

"My intense interests and different perspectives enrich my life and the lives of people who get to know me authentically."

"I can make choices based on my authentic needs and values rather than trying to meet others' expectations for how I should be."

Challenge-Specific Affirmations

For sensory sensitivities: *"My sensory needs are valid and important for my wellbeing. Taking care of these needs allows me to show up more fully in my relationships and activities."*

For social differences: *"I communicate and connect in ways that might be different but are equally valid. The right people will appreciate my authentic communication style."*

For executive function challenges: *"My brain has its own patterns and rhythms for accomplishing tasks. Working with these patterns rather than against them helps me be more effective."*

For masking recovery: *"I can choose when and how to share my authentic self rather than automatically performing neurotypical behavior. This choice gives me control over my energy and relationships."*

These discoveries guide us toward understanding how your authentic identity can flourish within your relationships and family connections. **The work of identity reconstruction creates the foundation for building relationships that truly know and appreciate who you are.**

Chapter 6: The Relationship Reset

Navigating Changes with Partners and Family

Discovering your AuDHD doesn't just change how you see yourself – it changes how you experience and navigate your closest relationships. The person your partner fell in love with, the child your parents raised, the friend others have known for years – that person was always authentically you, but they were also performing in ways that required enormous energy and sometimes prevented genuine intimacy.

When you begin unmasking and living more authentically, the people closest to you might feel confused, concerned, or even threatened by changes in your behavior and communication. They might wonder if you're becoming a different person, if your relationship is still solid, or if they ever really knew you at all.

This confusion is understandable. **Your loved ones have been in relationship with your masked self, and while that masked self was still genuinely you, it wasn't the complete picture.** As you begin expressing previously hidden aspects of your personality, needs, and communication style, your relationships will need to adjust and adapt.

The good news is that these adjustments, while sometimes challenging, often lead to deeper intimacy and more satisfying connections. **When you can be more authentic in your relationships, you create space for others to be more genuine as well.** The energy you were previously spending on masking becomes available for genuine presence and connection.

But this transition requires patience, clear communication, and strategic navigation of others' reactions and concerns. **The goal isn't to completely transform your relationships overnight, but to** gradually create space for more authenticity while maintaining the love and connection that drew you together in the first place.

Why Relationships Change Post-Diagnosis

Understanding why your relationships shift after AuDHD discovery helps both you and your loved ones navigate these changes with less anxiety and more intentional communication. **These changes aren't signs that your relationships were false before or that you're becoming a different person – they reflect the natural evolution that occurs when authenticity increases.**

The Energy Redistribution Effect

Before understanding your AuDHD, you likely spent significant mental and emotional energy managing your presentation in relationships – monitoring your responses, suppressing certain reactions, and working to appear neurotypical. **This energy expenditure affected not only how you showed up but also how much energy you had available for genuine connection and emotional presence.**

As you begin to unmask, this energy becomes available for deeper engagement with the people you care about. **You might find yourself more emotionally present, more able to focus on others' experiences, or more capable of handling relationship challenges because you're not simultaneously managing complex internal performances.**

A working professional might discover that after spending all day masking at work, they had little energy left for meaningful conversation with their partner in the evenings. **As they develop more sustainable approaches to workplace authenticity, they find themselves more emotionally available for their relationship, creating opportunities for deeper connection.**

However, this energy redistribution can also be confusing for partners who are used to certain patterns of interaction. **They might notice that you're more present in some ways but also more direct about** your needs, more willing to express disagreement, or less willing to accommodate requests that feel draining.

Authenticity's Impact on Communication

Your communication style might become more direct, honest, and efficient as you stop filtering everything through "How will this sound?" and start expressing your genuine thoughts and feelings. **This can feel refreshing and more intimate to some loved ones, while others might experience it as jarring or concerning.**

You might find yourself expressing enthusiasm about your interests more freely, asking for what you need more directly, or setting boundaries about activities and commitments that drain your energy. **These changes often represent healthier communication patterns, but they can feel unfamiliar to people who are used to your previous communication style.**

Your emotional expression might also become more authentic – perhaps you're more willing to express frustration when it arises rather than suppressing it, or you show genuine excitement about topics that matter to you instead of dampening your enthusiasm to avoid seeming "too much."

This increased emotional authenticity often leads to better emotional intimacy, but it can require adjustment from family members and partners who are used to more controlled or predictable emotional expressions.

Needs and Boundaries Clarification

As you understand your AuDHD better, you'll likely become clearer about your actual needs regarding sensory environments, social activities, communication styles, and energy management. **This clarity often leads to more specific requests and firmer boundaries, which can feel like significant changes to people who are used to your previous accommodation patterns.**

You might become less willing to attend social events that consistently drain your energy, more specific about your sensory needs in shared living spaces, or more direct about requesting downtime after stimulating activities. **These boundary changes are healthy and necessary, but they require adjustment and negotiation within your relationships.**

Your tolerance for certain relationship patterns might also change. **Conversations that feel meaningless, social obligations that serve others' needs but not yours, or relationship dynamics that require extensive masking might become less acceptable as you prioritize authenticity and energy management.**

Identity Integration in Relationships

As you integrate your AuDHD understanding into your sense of self, you might find that your priorities, interests, and relationship preferences shift in ways that affect your connections with others. **This doesn't mean your fundamental values or love for important people changes, but the ways you express these values and participate in relationships might need adjustment.**

You might discover that certain shared activities were more about accommodation than genuine interest, or that some relationship patterns were more about avoiding conflict than creating genuine connection. **As you become more authentic, you'll naturally gravitate toward interactions and activities that feel more aligned with your genuine self.**

This shift can create opportunities for deeper connection with people who appreciate and enjoy your authentic self, while potentially creating distance in relationships that were primarily sustained through accommodation and performance.

Explaining "I'm Not Different, I'm Just Honest Now"

One of the most important conversations you'll have with loved ones involves helping them understand that your increasing authenticity doesn't represent you becoming a different person. **You're becoming more honest about who you've always been, but haven't felt safe or understood enough to express fully.**

Addressing the "Sudden Change" Perception

Family members and partners might express concern that you're "suddenly" different or that your AuDHD discovery is causing you to change your personality. **Help them understand that these traits and preferences have always been part of who you are – you're just becoming more open about expressing them.**

You might explain that the behaviors they're noticing as "new" are actually behaviors you've been suppressing or modifying for years. **The stimming, the direct communication, the specific sensory needs, the intense interests – these have always been part of your authentic self, but you've learned to hide or modify them to fit social expectations.**

Use specific examples to illustrate this concept: "You know how I've always rearranged the living room furniture periodically? That's because certain arrangements help my brain feel more settled, but I never explained that before because I didn't understand it myself."

The goal is helping loved ones recognize continuities with your past behavior while understanding that you're now able to be more open about the reasons behind patterns they may have noticed but not understood.

Distinguishing Between Authentic and Reactive Changes

It's important to acknowledge that some changes in your behavior might be reactive rather than purely authentic – perhaps you're being more direct than feels natural because you're overcorrecting from years of accommodation, or you're being more rigid about boundaries than necessary because you're still learning to calibrate appropriate limits.

Help your loved ones understand the difference between your authentic self emerging and temporary adjustments as you figure out how to live more genuinely. Be willing to discuss which changes feel permanent and important versus which might be part of your adjustment process.

You might say something like: "I'm still figuring out how to balance being authentic with being considerate of others' needs. Some of these changes might feel extreme right now because I'm learning, but the core truth is that I need more honesty in our communication and more accommodation of my sensory and energy needs."

This acknowledgment helps loved ones feel included in your growth process rather than being surprised by sudden changes they don't understand.

Emphasizing Continuity in Love and Commitment

Make sure to clearly communicate that your increasing authenticity doesn't change your fundamental feelings about the important people in your life. **Your love, commitment, and care for family members and partners remain constant even as the ways you express these feelings might become more genuine.**

You might need to explicitly state: "My love for you hasn't changed at all. If anything, being able to be more honest about who I am makes it possible for me to love you more authentically and with more energy available for our relationship."

Help your loved ones understand that authenticity enhances rather than threatens your relationships. When you don't have to spend energy managing your presentation, you have more energy available for genuine care, attention, and emotional connection.

Address specific concerns about commitment by explaining how understanding your AuDHD actually supports your ability to be a better partner, parent, or family member because you can work with your brain's patterns rather than fighting against them constantly.

Inviting Them Into Your Experience

Rather than just explaining changes in your behavior, invite your loved ones to understand your internal experience and the energy costs of masking that they may not have realized you were managing.

Help them understand what daily life felt like when you were constantly monitoring and adjusting your behavior to appear neurotypical. Explain the exhaustion, the internal conflict, and the disconnection from your authentic self that masking created.

You might share specific examples: "When we go to parties, I spend the entire time monitoring my conversation topics, my body language, and my energy level to make sure I seem appropriately social. By the time we get home, I'm completely exhausted – not from the social interaction itself, but from the performance I was maintaining."

This sharing helps loved ones understand that your changes are about reducing unnecessary stress and energy expenditure, not about becoming less caring or committed to your relationships.

Managing Partner Confusion and Concerns

Romantic partners often experience the most complex reactions to your post-diagnosis changes because they've been most intimate with your masked self and might feel uncertain about how these changes affect your relationship dynamic and future plans.

Addressing Identity and Attraction Concerns

Partners might worry that if you're changing how you express yourself, their attraction to you or compatibility with you might be affected. **These concerns are natural but often based on misunderstanding about what's actually changing versus what's becoming more visible.**

Help your partner understand that your core personality, values, and ways of loving haven't changed – but the energy you have available for the relationship and the authenticity you can bring to it are likely to improve. **You're not becoming a different person; you're becoming a more relaxed and genuine version of yourself.**

Address attraction concerns directly: "The things you love about me – my sense of humor, my caring nature, my intelligence, my loyalty – those haven't changed. But you might notice that I express these qualities more freely and with less anxiety about whether I'm doing it 'right.'"

Some partners find that they're actually more attracted to their loved one's authentic self than they were to the masked version, even if the adjustment period involves some uncertainty and learning.

Processing Their Own Relationship History

Partners might need to process their own feelings about having been in relationship with someone who was masking significant aspects of their experience. **They might feel confused about which parts of your relationship history were "real" versus performed, or wonder if they ever truly knew you.**

Help them understand that the love, care, and connection you shared were always genuine, even when the expression of these feelings was filtered through masking behaviors. **The emotions were real; it was only the presentation that was modified to seem more neurotypical.**

You might explain: "All the times I showed love and care for you, all our meaningful conversations, all the fun we had together – those were completely real. The only thing that was different was that I was working harder than you realized to present myself in ways I thought you would find acceptable."

Reassure your partner that understanding your AuDHD actually makes it possible for them to know you more completely and authentically than they were able to before.

Navigating Changes in Relationship Dynamics

Your partner might need to adjust their expectations about social activities, communication patterns, household responsibilities, and daily routines as you begin accommodating your AuDHD needs more consciously.

Work together to identify which relationship patterns were working well for both of you versus which were primarily about

your accommodation of neurotypical expectations. Some changes might actually benefit your partner as well – perhaps you'll both enjoy social activities more when you choose them based on mutual preference rather than social obligation.

Be willing to negotiate and experiment with new approaches rather than making unilateral changes. **Your increasing authenticity should enhance your relationship, not create a situation where your needs are met at the expense of your partner's comfort and preferences.**

You might say: "I'd like us to figure out social and household patterns that work better for my energy management. This doesn't mean we can't do things you enjoy – let's find ways to make these activities work for both of us."

Building New Intimacy Patterns

As you become more authentic, you and your partner have the opportunity to develop new patterns of emotional and physical intimacy based on your actual preferences and needs rather than assumed neurotypical norms.

This might involve more direct communication about your needs, different approaches to physical affection that account for sensory preferences, or new ways of spending quality time together that feel energizing rather than draining for both of you.

Your partner might discover aspects of intimacy with you that weren't fully available when you were masking – perhaps deeper intellectual connection, more genuine emotional sharing, or physical intimacy that's more attuned to your actual sensory preferences.

The goal is building intimacy patterns that honor both your authentic self and your partner's needs and preferences, creating a relationship dynamic that supports both of your wellbeing and satisfaction.

Renegotiating Household Roles and Responsibilities

Living together requires practical negotiations about how daily life is organized, and your AuDHD understanding often reveals opportunities for more sustainable and equitable arrangements that work better for everyone involved.

Understanding Executive Function Realities

Your partner and family members might need education about how executive function differences affect your ability to handle certain household responsibilities, and how environmental factors influence your functioning in daily tasks.

Help them understand that struggles with certain tasks aren't about laziness, lack of caring, or unwillingness to contribute, but about genuine differences in how your brain processes and organizes information.

You might explain: "I want to contribute equally to our household, but I need us to organize responsibilities in ways that work with how my brain functions rather than against it. This might mean I take on different tasks than we originally assigned, or that I handle tasks at different times or in different ways."

Be specific about which types of tasks feel manageable versus overwhelming for you, and suggest alternative ways to contribute that align better with your strengths and energy patterns.

Playing to Strengths Rather Than Compensating for Weaknesses

Instead of focusing on accommodating your challenges, work together to identify household contributions that align with your AuDHD strengths and interests. **This approach often leads to better outcomes for everyone because you're contributing from areas of genuine capability and engagement.**

Perhaps you excel at organizing systems, researching major purchases, managing finances, maintaining outdoor spaces, or handling technology needs for the household. **These contributions** might be more valuable and sustainable than struggling to maintain neurotypical approaches to tasks that consistently drain your energy.

You might find that you can contribute more effectively by taking on larger responsibilities that match your interests and abilities rather than splitting every task evenly. **For example, you might handle all the meal planning and grocery shopping while your partner handles daily cooking, or you might manage all household maintenance while your partner handles social scheduling.**

Creating Sustainable Systems

Work together to create household management systems that account for your sensory needs, energy patterns, and executive function differences while still meeting the practical needs of everyone in the household.

This might involve environmental modifications that make tasks easier for you, scheduling adjustments that align with your natural energy rhythms, or organizational systems that work with your brain's patterns rather than fighting against them.

Consider how your sensory sensitivities affect household tasks and find accommodations that make these tasks more manageable. **This might mean using different cleaning products, organizing storage in visually clear ways, or scheduling noisy tasks for times when they won't be overwhelming.**

The goal is creating household systems that support everyone's wellbeing and effectiveness rather than requiring anyone to constantly fight against their natural patterns and preferences.

Handling Resistance and Negotiation

Some family members might resist changes to established household patterns, especially if they don't understand why changes are necessary or if they perceive changes as unfair or inconvenient.

Be prepared to explain not just what you need to change, but why these changes benefit the household overall. When you're working with your natural patterns rather than fighting against them, you're typically more effective, less stressed, and more emotionally available for your relationships.

Be willing to negotiate and experiment with different approaches rather than insisting on immediate complete accommodation. **You might try new arrangements on a trial basis, allowing everyone to adjust gradually and make modifications based on what actually works in practice.**

Address concerns about fairness by emphasizing that equal contribution doesn't necessarily mean identical contribution. **The goal is for everyone to contribute meaningfully in ways that align with their abilities and circumstances.**

Intimacy and Connection with AuDHD

Understanding your AuDHD opens up new possibilities for genuine intimacy and connection in your relationships, but it might also require adjustments to how you and your loved ones approach physical and emotional closeness.

Emotional Intimacy Adjustments

Your capacity for emotional intimacy might actually increase as you unmask because you have more energy available for genuine emotional connection and less need to monitor and modify your emotional expressions.

You might find yourself able to share thoughts and feelings more directly, respond to your loved ones' emotions more authentically, and create deeper understanding through honest communication about your internal experience.

However, your emotional processing and expression patterns might be different from neurotypical norms in ways that require education and adjustment from your loved ones. **You might need more time to process complex emotions, prefer to discuss feelings in specific** ways, or show care and love through actions that might not be immediately recognizable as affectionate.

Help your loved ones understand your authentic emotional patterns: "I show love by making sure you're comfortable and have what you need, even though I might not express affection in traditional ways. When I share detailed information about my interests with you, that's actually me trying to connect and include you in something that matters to me."

Physical Intimacy Considerations

Your sensory sensitivities and preferences affect physical intimacy in ways that might require communication and accommodation from partners. **Understanding and accommodating these preferences often leads to more satisfying physical connection for both partners.**

Be direct about sensory preferences that affect physical closeness – perhaps certain textures, temperatures, pressures, or types of touch feel particularly good or particularly uncomfortable. **This information helps your partner understand how to create physical experiences that feel good for both of you.**

You might discover that some physical activities that seemed problematic were actually about timing, environment, or approach rather than fundamental incompatibility. **Sensory-aware approaches to physical intimacy often enhance pleasure and comfort for both partners.**

Communication about physical preferences should be ongoing rather than a one-time conversation, as your awareness of your preferences develops and your needs might vary based on your sensory state and energy levels.

Social Intimacy Patterns

The ways you prefer to spend social time together might need adjustment based on your understanding of your energy management needs and social processing differences.

This might involve finding activity patterns that feel connecting rather than draining, communication approaches that feel genuine rather than performed, or social participation levels that you can sustain without exhaustion.

You might discover new ways of spending time together that feel more intimate because they don't require you to maintain social performances. **Perhaps you connect better during shared activities that don't require constant conversation, or you feel closest during quiet parallel activities rather than interactive social time.**

Help your loved ones understand that your social intimacy preferences aren't about wanting distance from them, but about finding ways to be together that allow you to be fully present rather than managing social performance.

Building Understanding and Accommodation

The key to successful intimacy adjustments is ongoing communication, experimentation, and mutual accommodation rather than expecting immediate perfect understanding from your loved ones.

Be willing to educate your partners and family members about your needs while also being open to learning about their needs and finding approaches that work for everyone involved.

Celebrate successful intimacy experiences that honor your AuDHD needs – these positive experiences help build confidence and understanding for both you and your loved ones about what authentic connection looks like in your relationships.

Relationship Impact Assessment

Before making changes in your relationships, it's helpful to systematically assess how your current relationship patterns align with your authentic needs and which areas might benefit from adjustment.

Energy Pattern Analysis

Track how different relationship activities and interactions affect your energy levels over time. **Notice which relationship experiences leave you feeling energized versus drained, and which activities you find yourself avoiding or dreading.**

Pay attention to whether your energy patterns in relationships change based on your masking level – do you feel more or less connected when you're being more authentic versus when you're managing your presentation carefully?

Consider how much energy you currently spend managing your presentation in different relationships, and how this energy expenditure affects your capacity for genuine connection and emotional availability.

Document which relationships feel most accepting of your authentic self versus those that seem to require more performance and accommodation from you.

Communication Effectiveness Review

Evaluate how effectively you're able to communicate your actual thoughts, feelings, and needs in different relationships. **Notice where communication feels natural and understood versus where you feel like you're constantly translating between your internal experience and what others seem to expect.**

Consider which relationships involve mutual sharing of authentic experiences versus those where the emotional labor feels unbalanced or where you're doing most of the accommodating.

Pay attention to which communication styles feel most genuine for you and how different people respond to your more direct communication approaches.

Assess whether your current communication patterns in relationships are sustainable long-term or whether they require energy expenditure that's contributing to stress and exhaustion.

Boundary and Accommodation Patterns

Examine your current patterns of boundary-setting and accommodation in relationships. **Notice which boundaries feel important for your wellbeing versus which you've set out of habit or social expectation.**

Consider which accommodations you make for others feel reasonable and reciprocal versus those that consistently drain your energy or require you to suppress important aspects of your authentic self.

Evaluate whether your current relationship patterns include appropriate accommodation of your sensory, social, and energy management needs, or whether you've been primarily focused on accommodating others' expectations.

Review which relationships include mutual flexibility and accommodation versus those where you're doing most of the adjusting to maintain harmony.

Communication Scripts for Partners

Clear, direct communication about your AuDHD discovery and its impact on your relationship helps partners understand what's changing and how they can support your authenticity while maintaining connection.

Initial Disclosure Scripts

"I've discovered that I have both autism and ADHD traits, which explains many of the differences I've always felt but couldn't name. This doesn't change how I feel about you or our relationship, but it helps me understand why certain things feel challenging for me and why I need specific accommodations to function at my best."

"Learning about my AuDHD has been both relieving and overwhelming. I'm still the same person who loves you, but I'm beginning to understand needs I've had my whole life that I've been trying to manage without understanding them. I'd like to share this

discovery with you and talk about how it might affect our relationship in positive ways."

"I want you to know that I've been masking many of my natural traits to seem more neurotypical, and this has been exhausting. As I become more authentic, you might notice some changes in my behavior, but these changes represent me becoming more honest about who I've always been rather than becoming a different person."

Ongoing Communication Scripts

"I need some time to process this conversation/situation before I can respond thoughtfully. This isn't about avoiding the discussion – it's about making sure I can engage authentically rather than just reacting."

"This environment/activity is overwhelming for my sensory system right now. Can we make some adjustments or take a break so I can be more present with you?"

"I'm feeling the need to engage with my special interest right now because it helps me regulate my emotions and energy. This isn't about avoiding you – it's about taking care of myself so I can be more available for our relationship."

"I realize I've been accommodating this situation in ways that aren't sustainable for me. Can we discuss some alternatives that might work better for both of us?"

Conflict Resolution Scripts

"I think we might be approaching this issue differently because of our different neurological styles. Can we talk about what each of us needs to feel heard and find a solution that works for both of us?"

"I need to be more direct about my feelings than I've been in the past. This isn't meant to be hurtful – it's my way of being honest so we can address issues before they become bigger problems."

"I'm feeling overwhelmed by this conflict right now. Can we take a break and return to this discussion when I can think more clearly? This will help me participate more constructively."

"I realize that my way of expressing frustration might seem intense. I'm working on communicating my needs before I become overwhelmed, but I need your patience as I learn better ways to handle difficult conversations."

Conflict Resolution Strategies

Relationship conflicts often require different approaches when one or both partners have AuDHD traits. **These strategies account for differences in communication style, emotional processing, and conflict tolerance that might not be addressed by conventional relationship advice.**

Preventing Overwhelm During Conflicts

Create agreements about how to handle conflicts when one person becomes overwhelmed or overstimulated. This might involve taking breaks, changing the environment, or using written communication instead of verbal discussion.

Recognize that conflict-related overwhelm isn't about avoiding responsibility or refusing to engage with problems. **It's about managing the neurological impacts of stress so that constructive problem-solving becomes possible.**

Develop signals or agreements about when someone needs to pause a conflict discussion for sensory or emotional regulation. **These pauses often lead to more productive problem-solving because both people can think more clearly.**

Consider whether the timing, environment, or approach to conflict discussions needs adjustment to accommodate sensory sensitivities or executive function differences.

Communication Style Accommodations

Work together to understand how different communication styles can be equally valid and effective, even if they don't match conventional relationship advice about conflict resolution.

Some people with AuDHD communicate most effectively about conflicts through writing, others through direct verbal discussion without emotional processing demands, and others through structured problem-solving approaches.

Be willing to experiment with different conflict resolution approaches rather than assuming that neurotypical communication norms will work best for your relationship.

Address concerns about directness or intensity by distinguishing between aggressive communication and honest communication that happens to be more intense than neurotypical norms.

Solution-Focused Problem Solving

Focus conflict resolution on identifying practical solutions rather than processing emotions extensively, especially when emotional processing feels overwhelming or unproductive for one or both people.

Some relationship conflicts are better resolved through environmental changes, system modifications, or practical accommodations rather than through extensive emotional discussion.

Be willing to address underlying systems and patterns that create recurring conflicts rather than just addressing individual incidents.

Consider whether certain conflicts reflect mismatches between neurological needs and current relationship patterns rather than fundamental relationship problems.

Intimacy Navigation Tools

Creating genuine intimacy when you have AuDHD often requires more intentional communication and accommodation than

conventional relationship advice suggests. These tools help you build connection approaches that work for your actual needs and preferences.

Sensory Intimacy Planning

Discuss sensory preferences and sensitivities that affect physical and emotional intimacy. This includes environmental factors like lighting, temperature, sound, and texture, as well as preferences for different types of physical contact.

Create intimacy environments that feel comfortable and appealing rather than overwhelming or distracting. **This might involve specific lighting, comfortable temperatures, preferred textures, or minimal sensory distractions.**

Be willing to communicate about sensory preferences without judgment or interpretation – these are neurological realities rather than relationship statements.

Experiment with timing intimacy for when your sensory system feels most regulated and receptive rather than forcing connection when you're feeling overwhelmed or understimulated.

Energy-Aware Connection

Plan intimate time based on both partners' energy patterns rather than assuming that spontaneous intimacy is always preferable. Some people connect better when they can prepare mentally and emotionally for intimate interaction.

Consider how masking and social energy expenditure affect your capacity for intimacy, and plan accordingly. **You might connect more authentically when you haven't been spending energy on social performance earlier in the day.**

Recognize that different types of intimacy require different amounts of energy, and that your capacity for various types of connection might vary based on your overall energy levels.

Develop multiple approaches to intimacy that work for different energy levels and circumstances rather than having only one pattern that might not always be accessible.

Communication-Based Intimacy

For many people with AuDHD, intellectual and communicative connection provides a foundation for other types of intimacy. Sharing interests, discussing ideas, and engaging in detailed conversation about meaningful topics can create deep bonding.

Be willing to share your special interests as a form of intimacy – when you include others in topics that fascinate you, you're offering them access to an important part of your inner world.

Recognize that different people express love and care in different ways, and learn to interpret your partner's expressions of affection even if they don't match neurotypical norms.

Practice communicating appreciation for the specific ways your partner shows care and connection, even if these expressions are subtle or unconventional.

These discoveries lead us naturally to the broader context of family relationships and the complex decisions involved in sharing your AuDHD discovery with extended family members who may have varying levels of understanding and acceptance of neurodivergent experiences.

Chapter 7: Family Dynamics and Disclosure

Telling Your Story, Setting Boundaries

Deciding how much to share about your AuDHD discovery with family members involves complex considerations that go far beyond simply providing information. **Family relationships carry decades of shared history, established patterns, and emotional investments that can make disclosure both more meaningful and more complicated than sharing with friends or colleagues.**

Unlike other relationships where you might choose your level of connection based on mutual compatibility and understanding, family relationships often involve ongoing contact regardless of how well individuals understand or accept your neurodivergent identity. **This reality makes strategic thinking about disclosure particularly important – you want to share authentically while protecting your wellbeing and maintaining relationships that matter to you.**

Family members might respond to your AuDHD disclosure with everything from genuine curiosity and support to skepticism, denial, or attempts to minimize your experience. **These varied reactions often reflect their own comfort levels with difference, their understanding of neurodivergence, and their investment in maintaining existing family dynamics rather than their feelings about you personally.**

The goal of family disclosure isn't to achieve universal acceptance or understanding – it's to create space for more authentic relationships with family members who are capable of growth and connection, while maintaining appropriate boundaries with those who aren't ready or able to support your authentic self.

Some family members will surprise you with their understanding and acceptance. Others might need time and education to adjust their understanding of you. **And some might never fully accept your neurodivergent identity – learning to navigate all these responses while maintaining your own wellbeing is a crucial skill for long-term family harmony.**

Deciding Who to Tell and When

Not all family members need the same level of information about your AuDHD discovery, and not all need to be told at the same time or in the same way. Strategic disclosure involves considering each relationship individually and making conscious choices about what to share based on your specific circumstances and goals.

Assessing Family Relationship Safety

Before disclosing to any family member, honestly assess the current state of your relationship and their likely capacity to handle neurodivergent information constructively. **This assessment helps you make informed decisions about what level of disclosure feels appropriate and safe.**

Consider each family member's history of responding to differences or challenges. **Have they shown flexibility and growth when presented with new information about family members? Do they tend to be supportive during difficult times, or do they minimize problems and push for "normalcy"?**

Think about their current understanding of mental health, disabilities, or neurodivergence. **Family members who already have some familiarity with autism or ADHD might be more prepared to understand AuDHD, while those who view these as "excuses" or "trends" might require more careful approach or might not be safe for full disclosure.**

Evaluate the power dynamics in your relationship with each family member. **Parents, older siblings, or family members who provide financial or practical support might have more influence over** your life circumstances, making disclosure decisions more complex.

Consider your emotional relationship with each person. **Family members who have consistently shown care and concern for your wellbeing are more likely to respond supportively to disclosure, while those with whom you have strained or competitive relationships might use the information in ways that aren't helpful.**

Timing Considerations

The timing of family disclosure can significantly affect how the information is received and processed. Consider both your own readiness and external circumstances that might influence family members' capacity to respond thoughtfully.

Make sure you feel reasonably stable in your own understanding of your AuDHD before sharing with family members. **If you're still processing complex emotions about your discovery or feeling uncertain about your own identity, you might want to work through some of these feelings before managing others' reactions as well.**

Consider whether family members are dealing with their own stresses or life changes that might affect their ability to focus on your disclosure. **Major illnesses, job changes, relationship problems, or other family crises might not be ideal times for sharing complex personal information.**

Avoid disclosure during emotionally charged family gatherings or events where your information might get lost in other dynamics or where privacy for processing reactions isn't available.

Think about whether you want to tell multiple family members simultaneously or individually. **Individual conversations often allow for more personalized approaches and deeper discussion, while group disclosure might create more support but also more complex dynamics.**

Level of Detail Decisions

Different family members might need different amounts of information about your AuDHD discovery. Consider what level of detail serves both your authenticity goals and the relationship dynamics with each person.

Some family members might benefit from comprehensive education about AuDHD, including information about how it explains patterns they've observed in your behavior throughout your life. **These conversations might involve sharing resources, answering detailed questions, and ongoing discussion as everyone adjusts to this new understanding.**

Others might need only basic information that helps them understand why you might have different needs or preferences without requiring them to become experts in neurodivergence. **For these relationships, simple explanations focused on practical implications might be most effective.**

Consider which family members would be interested in learning about your internal experience versus those who primarily need to understand external accommodations or changes in your behavior.

Some family members might not need any detailed information about your AuDHD, but might benefit from knowing that you've gained new understanding about yourself that explains some of your differences and needs.

Managing Your Own Expectations

Before disclosing to family members, get clear about what you're hoping to achieve and what would constitute a positive outcome from your perspective. Realistic expectations help prevent disappointment and guide your approach to each conversation.

Consider whether you're primarily seeking understanding, accommodation, closer connection, or simply transparency about who you are. **These different goals might require different approaches and create different measures of success.**

Be prepared for the possibility that some family members might not respond as positively as you hope, while others might be more understanding than you expected. **Family members often surprise us in both directions.**

Remember that initial reactions might not represent long-term responses. Some family members need time to process new information and might become more understanding over time, while others might initially seem supportive but struggle with ongoing accommodation.

Consider what you'll do if disclosure doesn't lead to the understanding or connection you're hoping for. **Having plans for maintaining your wellbeing regardless of family responses helps you approach disclosure from a position of strength rather than dependency.**

Scripts for Different Family Members

Different family relationships require different approaches to disclosure, taking into account the unique dynamics, history, and communication patterns you have with each person. These scripts provide starting points that you can adapt to your specific relationships and circumstances.

Parents and Caregivers

Parents often have the most complex responses to adult children's neurodivergent discoveries because they might feel responsible for not recognizing signs earlier or might need to process their own experiences of parenting a neurodivergent child without understanding.

"I've learned something important about myself that I'd like to share with you. I've discovered that I have both autism and ADHD traits, which explains many of the differences and challenges I've experienced throughout my life. This isn't about blame or wondering

'what if' – it's about finally understanding myself better and being able to take better care of my needs."

"I know this might be surprising information, and you might have questions or concerns. I want you to know that this discovery has been positive for me – it's helped me understand why certain things have always felt difficult and why I need specific accommodations to function at my best. I'm still your child, and I still value our relationship, but I'd like to be more honest about who I am."

"I realize you might be wondering if there were signs you missed or things you could have done differently. Please know that you did the best you could with the understanding available at the time. The important thing now is that we all have better information to understand and support each other."

Siblings

Sibling relationships often involve complex dynamics of comparison, competition, and shared history that can affect how neurodivergent disclosure is received and processed.

"I've discovered something about myself that explains a lot about our childhood and why I always seemed to respond to things differently than you did. I have autism and ADHD traits, which means my brain processes information and experiences differently. This doesn't change how I feel about our relationship, but it might help you understand some of the patterns you noticed growing up."

"I wanted to share this with you because our relationship matters to me, and I'd like to be more authentic about who I am. If you've ever wondered why I seemed to struggle with things that came easily to you, or why I was so intense about certain interests, this information might provide some context."

"I know we've had our conflicts over the years, and I'm not trying to use this as an excuse for anything. But understanding my neurodivergence has helped me realize that some of our misunderstandings might have been about different ways of *processing and responding to situations rather than fundamental personality conflicts."*

Extended Family

Grandparents, aunts, uncles, and cousins might need simpler explanations focused on practical implications rather than detailed education about neurodivergence.

"I've learned that I have some brain differences called autism and ADHD that explain why I've always needed quiet time, had intense interests, and been sensitive to certain environments. I'm sharing this because I want you to understand that these aren't personality flaws or choices – they're just how my brain works."

"You might notice that I approach social gatherings or family events a bit differently now that I understand my needs better. This isn't about not wanting to spend time with family – it's about participating in ways that work better for how my brain functions."

"I hope you'll be patient with me as I learn to be more honest about my needs. Sometimes I might need to take breaks from noisy environments, or I might be more direct about what works and doesn't work for me. This is about taking better care of myself so I can be more present with all of you."

Adult Children

If you're sharing your AuDHD discovery with your own adult children, they might be processing not only your disclosure but also wondering about their own neurodivergent traits or reflecting on their childhood experiences.

"I've learned something about myself that I want to share with you, and that might also explain some patterns in our family. I have autism and ADHD traits, which means I process information and experiences differently than neurotypical people. Looking back, this might explain some of the ways I approached parenting or the accommodations I needed."

"This discovery doesn't change how much I love you or how proud I am of you. If anything, it helps me understand why certain aspects of parenting felt particularly challenging or why I approached things differently than other parents might have."

"You might be wondering if this affects you, since neurodivergence can be hereditary. There's no pressure for you to explore this for yourself, but if you're curious about your own traits or experiences, I'm here to support you in whatever way feels helpful."

Managing Skepticism and Denial

Many family members might respond to your AuDHD disclosure with skepticism, denial, or attempts to minimize your experience. These reactions can be hurtful, but they often reflect the family member's own discomfort with neurodivergence concepts rather than accurate assessment of your experience.

Understanding Common Skeptical Responses

Family members might express skepticism in various ways: "Everyone's a little autistic," "You seem too normal to have ADHD," "This is just the latest trend," or "You're looking for excuses for your problems." **These responses often come from lack of understanding about neurodivergence rather than deliberate attempts to hurt you.**

Some family members might point to your achievements or apparent social skills as evidence that you can't be neurodivergent. Help them understand that neurodivergent people can be highly capable and successful while still having genuine differences in how they process information and manage daily life.

Others might compare you to stereotypical presentations of autism or ADHD and conclude that you don't "fit the mold." **Explain that neurodivergence presents differently in different people, and that many common stereotypes are based on outdated or incomplete understanding.**

Some family members might interpret your disclosure as criticism of how they parented, taught, or treated you, leading them to become defensive rather than curious. **Address these concerns directly by emphasizing that you're sharing information about yourself rather than making judgments about others.**

Responding to Denial Without Defensiveness

When family members deny or minimize your AuDHD experience, avoid getting pulled into arguments about whether your traits are "real" or significant enough to matter. Instead, focus on your experience and needs rather than trying to convince skeptical family members.

You might respond: "I understand this might be new information for you. I'm not asking you to become an expert in neurodivergence, but I would appreciate your support as I learn to take better care of my needs."

Avoid providing extensive evidence or documentation to prove your neurodivergence to skeptical family members. Your worth and the validity of your experience don't depend on their acceptance or understanding.

If family members continue to express skepticism, you might say: "I can see that you have concerns about this. I'm comfortable with my understanding of myself, and I hope we can focus on maintaining our relationship rather than debating my neurodivergence."

Set boundaries about how much time and energy you're willing to spend educating family members who seem resistant to learning. You can offer resources and answer questions, but you don't have to convince anyone of your legitimacy.

Dealing with Minimization

Family members might acknowledge your differences but minimize their significance with responses like "Everyone struggles with those things" or "You've managed fine so far, so it can't be that big a deal." **These responses often reflect discomfort with the implications of** your disclosure rather than accurate assessment of your experience.

Help family members understand that the fact that you've developed coping strategies doesn't mean the underlying differences aren't real or significant. Many neurodivergent people develop remarkable resilience and adaptation skills that mask the extent of their daily challenges.

You might explain: "The fact that I've found ways to manage doesn't mean the challenges weren't real or that the coping strategies weren't exhausting. Understanding my neurodivergence helps me find more sustainable approaches."

Address the "everyone struggles" response by acknowledging that while everyone has challenges, neurodivergent people often face additional layers of difficulty that aren't immediately visible to others.

If family members continue to minimize your experience, focus on your current needs rather than trying to convince them of past difficulties: "Regardless of how significant you think these differences are, I'm asking for specific accommodations that help me function better and maintain our relationship more effectively."

Setting Limits on Educational Labor

You are not obligated to educate resistant family members or to provide extensive proof of your neurodivergent experience. While some family members might benefit from education and resources, others might not be ready or willing to learn regardless of how much effort you invest.

Decide in advance how much time and energy you're willing to spend on education for each family member, and stick to those limits. **You might offer one or two resources, answer a few questions, but then redirect conversations if family members remain resistant or demanding.**

You might say: "I've shared some resources with you, and I'm happy to answer a few questions, but I can't spend ongoing energy trying to convince you. I hope you'll consider learning more on your own time if you're interested."

If family members demand extensive proof or become argumentative, you can end those conversations: "I'm not going to debate my own experience with you. If you'd like to understand better, there are resources available, but I'm not going to continue this conversation if it becomes adversarial."

Remember that your energy is better spent on relationships and activities that support your wellbeing rather than trying to change the minds of resistant family members.

Protecting Yourself from Invalidation

Family invalidation of your AuDHD experience can be particularly painful because these are relationships that carry deep emotional significance and long history. Developing strategies for protecting yourself from invalidation helps you maintain your sense of self while navigating complex family dynamics.

Recognizing Invalidation Patterns

Family invalidation might be obvious ("That's ridiculous" or "You're being dramatic") or subtle (changing the subject when you mention your needs, making jokes about your differences, or consistently "forgetting" your accommodations).

Some family members might express surface-level acceptance while consistently failing to accommodate your actual needs. They might say they understand but continue to plan family events in overwhelming environments or expect you to participate in activities that consistently drain your energy.

Others might acknowledge your differences but frame them as choices rather than neurological realities: "You could focus if you really tried" or "You just need to push yourself more." **These** responses reflect misunderstanding about the nature of neurodivergent differences.

Pay attention to family members who consistently redirect conversations away from your needs or who make your accommodation requests about their convenience rather than your wellbeing.

Building Internal Validation

The most important protection against family invalidation is developing strong internal validation of your own experience and needs. When you're confident in your self-understanding, others' skepticism becomes less destabilizing.

Keep records of your neurodivergent experiences and patterns so you have concrete evidence of your traits when self-doubt arises. **This isn't about proving yourself to others, but about maintaining your own clarity when others question your reality.**

Connect with neurodivergent communities and professionals who understand AuDHD experiences. **Having relationships where your neurodivergence is accepted and understood provides balance against family relationships where it might be questioned.**

Develop clear language for your own needs and boundaries so you can communicate them confidently regardless of others' reactions. **The clearer you are about your needs, the less likely you are to be swayed by others' invalidation.**

Practice self-compassion when family members' responses are disappointing. Their inability to understand or accept your neurodivergence reflects their limitations, not your worth or the validity of your experience.

Strategic Information Sharing

Not all family members deserve access to detailed information about your internal experiences, struggles, or needs. Share information strategically based on each person's demonstrated capacity to handle it supportively.

Some family members might get basic information about your accommodations needs: "I need quiet environments to function well," without detailed explanations of your sensory processing differences.

Others might earn access to more personal information through their supportive responses and genuine interest in understanding your experience.

Don't feel obligated to justify your needs or provide extensive explanations to family members who consistently respond with skepticism or invalidation. **Simple statements about what you need are sufficient for people who aren't genuinely trying to understand.**

If family members demand explanations or proof, you can redirect: "I'm not going to justify my needs to you. This is how I function best, and I'm asking for your cooperation rather than your analysis."

Creating Support Systems

Build relationships outside your family that provide the understanding and acceptance that might not be available from all family members. This support helps you maintain perspective when family relationships become invalidating.

Consider working with a neurodivergent-affirming therapist who can help you process family dynamics and develop strategies for maintaining your wellbeing in challenging family relationships.

Connect with other adults who have navigated similar family disclosure experiences. Their perspectives and strategies can be invaluable for managing your own family dynamics.

Develop friendships and community connections that celebrate and support your authentic self so you're not dependent solely on family acceptance for validation.

Make sure you have safe spaces and relationships where you can be completely authentic without having to justify or explain your neurodivergent traits.

Building Supportive Family Systems

While not all family members will become fully understanding of your AuDHD experience, many families can develop more supportive patterns with education, clear communication, and consistent boundaries. The goal is creating family dynamics that accommodate your needs while maintaining meaningful connections.

Gradual Education Approaches

For family members who show genuine interest in understanding your AuDHD experience, provide education gradually rather than overwhelming them with information all at once. Start with basic concepts and build understanding over time.

Share articles, videos, or books that explain AuDHD in accessible language. **Resources created by neurodivergent people themselves often provide more accurate and nuanced information than clinical descriptions.**

Be willing to answer questions and provide clarification, but set limits on how much educational labor you're willing to do. **Family members who are genuinely interested will often do their own research once you provide initial direction.**

Use concrete examples from your own experience to help family members understand how AuDHD affects daily life. Personal examples often make abstract concepts more understandable and relatable.

Acknowledge and appreciate family members who make efforts to learn and accommodate your needs, even if their understanding isn't perfect. **Positive reinforcement encourages continued growth and learning.**

Accommodation Negotiation

Work with receptive family members to develop practical accommodations that support your wellbeing during family interactions and events. Focus on specific, actionable changes rather than abstract understanding.

This might involve modifying family gathering environments (lighting, noise levels, seating arrangements), adjusting communication patterns (more direct requests, written information), or changing activity planning (advance notice, quieter alternatives, flexible participation).

Be specific about what accommodations are most important versus what would be nice but isn't essential. This helps family members prioritize their accommodation efforts.

Be willing to suggest alternatives rather than just identifying problems. **If traditional family activities don't work well for you, propose modified versions that might work better for everyone.**

Acknowledge that some accommodations might require adjustment from other family members, and be willing to negotiate solutions that work for multiple people rather than demanding unilateral changes.

Boundary Enforcement

Clear, consistent boundaries help family members understand your limits while maintaining relationships that are important to you. These boundaries protect your wellbeing and teach family members how to interact with you respectfully.

Be specific about consequences for boundary violations rather than making threats you're not prepared to follow through on. **This might mean leaving events early, limiting contact, or declining participation in activities that consistently ignore your needs.**

Distinguish between boundaries that are negotiable versus non-negotiable based on your wellbeing needs. **Some accommodations might have flexibility while others are essential for your ability to participate at all.**

Communicate boundaries clearly and calmly rather than during conflicts or emotionally charged moments. Family members are more likely to respect limits when they're presented as information rather than ultimatums.

Be prepared to enforce boundaries consistently even when it's inconvenient or creates conflict. **Family members learn to respect your limits through your consistent responses rather than your explanations.**

Long-term Relationship Building

Building supportive family systems is often a long-term process that requires patience and consistent effort from both you and family members who are willing to grow. Focus on progress rather than perfection.

Celebrate small improvements and positive changes in family members' understanding and accommodation. **Acknowledging growth encourages continued development and shows appreciation for their efforts.**

Be willing to adjust your approach based on what works best with each family member. Some people learn through discussion, others through reading, and others through observing positive changes in your wellbeing.

Accept that some family relationships might improve significantly while others remain limited in their capacity for understanding and accommodation. **This variability is normal and doesn't reflect failure on anyone's part.**

Focus your energy on family relationships that show potential for growth while maintaining appropriate boundaries with those that consistently drain your resources or invalidate your experience.

Disclosure Decision Matrix

Making strategic decisions about family disclosure involves weighing multiple factors for each relationship. This matrix helps you think through the considerations systematically rather than making decisions based solely on emotion or obligation.

High-Support, High-Safety Relationships

These are family members who have consistently shown support for you during challenges, demonstrated flexibility and growth, and maintain safe emotional boundaries in your relationship.

These relationships are often good candidates for comprehensive disclosure including detailed information about your AuDHD experience, your needs and accommodations, and the impact of masking on your energy and wellbeing.

Family members in this category might become allies in helping you navigate other family relationships or creating more accommodating family dynamics overall.

The risk in these relationships is relatively low, and the potential benefits of authenticity and support are high.

High-Support, Moderate-Safety Relationships

These family members care about your wellbeing but might have limited understanding of neurodivergence or might struggle with change and new information.

These relationships might benefit from gradual disclosure with basic information followed by more detailed sharing based on their responses and interest in learning.

Be prepared to provide more education and patience while these family members adjust their understanding of you and neurodivergence.

The potential for growth in these relationships is good, but it might require more time and effort from you.

Low-Support, High-Safety Relationships

Some family members might not be particularly supportive but also aren't actively harmful or invalidating. They might simply be emotionally unavailable or focused on their own lives.

These relationships might need only basic information – perhaps just enough explanation to help them understand any changes in your behavior or participation in family activities.

Don't expect significant accommodation or support from these family members, but they might not actively oppose your authenticity either.

The goal with these relationships is often simply maintaining cordial connection without expecting deep understanding or significant support.

Low-Support, Low-Safety Relationships

Family members who have a history of being critical, invalidating, or using personal information against you during conflicts require the most careful consideration.

These relationships might not be appropriate for any detailed disclosure about your AuDHD experience, especially if you depend on these family members for practical support or if disclosure might create additional family conflict.

Consider whether any information sharing is necessary or beneficial, or whether these relationships might function better with minimal personal disclosure.

The priority in these relationships is protecting your wellbeing rather than achieving understanding or authenticity.

Age-Appropriate Explanations for Children

When sharing your AuDHD discovery with children in your family – your own children, nieces and nephews, or grandchildren – the explanation needs to be tailored to their developmental stage and relationship with you. The goal is helping them understand any changes they might notice while providing age-appropriate information about neurodivergence.

Early Childhood (Ages 3-7)

Young children need simple, concrete explanations that focus on observable differences rather than complex concepts about neurodivergence.

"You know how some people wear glasses because their eyes work differently? My brain works a little differently too, which means I need certain things to help me feel comfortable and happy. Sometimes I might need quiet time, or I might get excited about things I'm interested in."

"I learned something new about myself that explains why I sometimes need to use my special headphones or why I like things to be organized in certain ways. These aren't weird things – they're just things that help my brain work better."

Focus on reassurance that your differences don't change your relationship with them: *"I'm still the same person who loves you very much. Learning about how my brain works just helps me take better care of myself so I can be the best [parent/grandparent/aunt/uncle] I can be."*

Middle Childhood (Ages 8-12)

Children in this age range can understand more complex concepts and might be curious about the specifics of neurodivergence, especially if they've learned about differences and disabilities at school.

"I've learned that I have something called autism and ADHD, which means my brain processes information differently than some other people's brains. This explains why I've always been really interested in [specific interests] and why I sometimes need quiet time or have strong reactions to loud noises."

"You might have noticed that I do some things differently than other adults – like how I organize things in very specific ways or how I sometimes get really focused on projects. Now I understand that these are part of how my brain works, and they're not good or bad things – they're just different."

Encourage questions and curiosity: *"Do you have any questions about this? I'm happy to explain anything you're wondering about. Some kids also have brains that work in similar ways, and that's completely okay too."*

Adolescence (Ages 13-18)

Teenagers can understand complex concepts and might be processing their own identity questions, making them potentially very interested in or concerned about neurodivergent traits.

"I want to share something I've learned about myself that might help explain some patterns you've noticed throughout your life. I have autism and ADHD traits, which means my brain processes sensory information, social situations, and attention differently than neurotypical people."

"This discovery has been really helpful for me because it explains why certain things have always felt challenging and why I need specific accommodations to function at my best. It doesn't change who I am – it just gives me language for differences I've always had."

Address potential concerns about heredity: *"You might be wondering if this affects you, since neurodivergence can run in families. There's no pressure to explore this for yourself, but if you ever have questions about your own experiences or traits, I'm here to support you."*

"Understanding my neurodivergence has actually made me a better parent because I can be more authentic and I have better strategies for managing stress and overwhelm."

Addressing Children's Concerns

Children of any age might worry that your AuDHD discovery changes your relationship with them or indicates that something is wrong. **Address these concerns directly and age-appropriately.**

Reassure them that neurodivergence isn't an illness or something that needs to be fixed: *"This isn't something that's wrong with me – it's just information about how my brain works. Lots of people have brains that work in different ways."*

Explain that understanding your AuDHD actually helps you be more present and available: *"Now that I understand my needs better, I can take better care of myself, which means I have more energy for spending time with you and doing things we both enjoy."*

If children express worry about having similar traits, provide reassurance without dismissing their concerns: *"If you ever think you might have a brain that works similarly to mine, that would be okay too. Different brains have different strengths, and we can figure out together what helps you feel your best."*

Extended Family Education Templates

Extended family members often need different approaches to education than immediate family members because the relationships are typically less intimate and the contact might be less frequent. These templates provide starting points for different types of extended family relationships.

Grandparents and Older Relatives

Older family members might have limited familiarity with current understanding of neurodivergence but often respond well to respectful education that connects to their own experiences and values.

"I wanted to let you know that I've learned something important about myself. I have conditions called autism and ADHD that explain why I've always been sensitive to noise, needed quiet time, and had intense interests in specific topics. This isn't a new thing – I've always been this way, but now I have words for it."

"I know these terms might be unfamiliar, but they basically mean my brain processes information differently than most people's brains. This explains why I sometimes need accommodations or why certain situations feel overwhelming for me."

"I hope you'll be patient with me as I learn to be more honest about my needs instead of just trying to push through difficult situations. This isn't about being difficult or demanding – it's about taking care of my health and wellbeing."

Aunts, Uncles, and Adult Cousins

Extended family members who are peers or near-peers might be interested in more detailed information and might be processing their own understanding of family patterns and traits.

"I've recently discovered that I have autism and ADHD traits, which explains a lot about my personality and needs that you might have noticed over the years. This discovery has been really positive because it helps me understand myself better and take better care of my needs."

"You might remember that I was always the kid who got overwhelmed at big family gatherings or who had really intense interests in specific topics. Understanding my neurodivergence helps me see that these were early signs of how my brain processes information differently."

"I'm sharing this with you because I value our relationship and I want to be more authentic about who I am. If you have questions or want to understand better, I'm happy to discuss it, but I also understand if this is new information that takes time to process."

Family Friends and Chosen Family

People who aren't biologically related but who function as family often respond differently than blood relatives because the relationships are chosen and might be more flexible.

"I want to share something with you that's been significant in my understanding of myself. I've learned that I have autism and ADHD, which explains many of the patterns and preferences you've probably noticed in how I navigate social situations and manage daily life."

"This discovery has been incredibly validating because it explains why I've always felt different in certain ways and why I need specific

accommodations to function comfortably. I'm sharing this with you because our relationship is important to me and I want you to understand this aspect of who I am."

"I hope this information helps you understand why I might need to approach social activities differently or why I might be more direct about my needs than I've been in the past. This isn't about pushing people away – it's about being more authentic so I can maintain better relationships with the people who matter to me."

Boundary Enforcement Guides

Clear boundaries help family members understand your limits and needs while protecting your energy and wellbeing. These guides provide specific language and strategies for maintaining boundaries with different types of family boundary violations.

Sensory Boundary Enforcement

When family members ignore or dismiss your sensory needs:

"I need to step outside/take a break/adjust the environment because the sensory input is becoming overwhelming for me. This isn't optional – it's what I need to do to take care of my nervous system."

"I've explained that I need [specific accommodation]. If this accommodation isn't possible, I'll need to [specific consequence like leaving early or participating differently]."

"I understand you might not understand why this sensory issue affects me so strongly, but I need you to respect that it does. I'm not asking you to understand – I'm asking you to accommodate."

Communication Boundary Enforcement

When family members invalidate or minimize your experience:

"I'm not going to continue this conversation if it becomes about whether my neurodivergence is real or significant. I'm sharing information about my experience, not asking for your analysis or approval."

"I need you to stop making jokes about my autism/ADHD traits. These comments are hurtful and they make it difficult for me to be authentic around you."

"I understand you might have different opinions about neurodivergence, but I need you to respect my understanding of my own experience. If you can't do that, we'll need to limit our discussions about this topic."

Participation Boundary Enforcement

When family members pressure you to participate in activities that don't accommodate your needs:

"I've explained that this type of event/activity doesn't work well for me. I'm not going to continue explaining why – I'm just letting you know that I won't be participating unless we can make some adjustments."

"I love spending time with the family, but I need us to find ways to connect that work for my energy and sensory needs. If traditional family activities can't be modified, I'll need to participate differently or less frequently."

"I'm not trying to be difficult or unsocial. I'm trying to participate in family activities in ways that are sustainable for me. This means I might need to leave early, take breaks, or decline certain activities altogether."

These principles direct our attention to the broader question of how to build and maintain friendships and community connections that support your authentic self while managing the complex social energy requirements that come with AuDHD traits.

Chapter 8: Friendship and Community

Finding Your People

Discovering your AuDHD often brings a new perspective on friendship that can be both liberating and challenging. **You might suddenly understand why certain friendships always felt exhausting, why you struggled to maintain social connections that seemed effortless for others, or why you felt lonely even when surrounded by people.**

At the same time, this new understanding opens up possibilities for more authentic connections. **When you know your social energy patterns, communication preferences, and authentic interests, you can build friendships that energize rather than drain you, and find communities where you belong rather than just fit in.**

The process of recalibrating your social life isn't always comfortable. **You might realize that some long-standing friendships were based more on mutual accommodation than genuine compatibility, while discovering that you're capable of deeper connections than you previously thought possible.**

Friendship with AuDHD isn't about having fewer social connections or isolating yourself from neurotypical people. It's about being strategic and intentional about where you invest your social energy so that your relationships contribute to your wellbeing rather than consistently draining your resources.

This recalibration often leads to a smaller but more satisfying social circle – friendships characterized by mutual understanding, shared interests that feel genuine rather than obligatory, and communication patterns that feel natural rather than performed. **The goal isn't to have** the most friends, but to have friendships that enhance your life and allow for authentic connection.

Why Friendships May Need Recalibration

Understanding your AuDHD changes not just how you see yourself, but how you understand the energy dynamics, communication patterns, and compatibility factors that make friendships sustainable and satisfying. **This new awareness often reveals mismatches between your actual social needs and your current friendship patterns.**

Energy Awareness and Social Battery Management

Before understanding your AuDHD, you might have pushed yourself to maintain social connections without recognizing the energy costs involved. **Many people describe feeling guilty about needing recovery time after social activities, or forcing themselves to participate in social events that consistently left them feeling drained.**

With AuDHD awareness comes recognition that your social energy operates differently than neurotypical patterns. You might need more recovery time between social activities, function better with predictable social plans rather than spontaneous gatherings, or find that certain types of social interaction energize you while others are exhausting.

A working professional might discover that they can enjoy dinner with a close friend who shares their interests but find cocktail parties with colleagues completely overwhelming. **This isn't about being antisocial – it's about recognizing which social activities align with your neurological patterns versus which require unsustainable energy expenditure.**

This awareness might lead you to reduce participation in social activities that consistently drain your energy without providing meaningful connection or enjoyment. **Some friends might interpret this as rejection or becoming "antisocial," when you're actually** becoming more selective about where you invest your limited social resources.

Unmasking Effects on Friendship Dynamics

As you begin to unmask and express your authentic self more freely, some friendships might shift in ways that feel uncomfortable or reveal incompatibilities that weren't previously obvious.

Friends who were comfortable with your masked self might feel confused or concerned when you begin expressing your genuine interests, communication style, or energy needs more directly. They might comment that you seem "different" or wonder if something is wrong with you or your friendship.

You might find yourself less willing to engage in conversations that feel meaningless, less able to tolerate social activities that overwhelm your sensory system, or more direct in your communication about your needs and preferences. **These changes often represent healthier social behaviors, but they can disrupt established friendship patterns.**

Some friends might appreciate your increased authenticity and find that the friendship becomes deeper and more genuine. Others might prefer the relationship dynamics that existed when you were masking more extensively. **Both responses are information about compatibility rather than judgments about anyone's worth as a person.**

Recognition of Compatibility Patterns

AuDHD awareness often brings clarity about which types of people and social situations genuinely work well for you versus which you've been tolerating or forcing yourself to enjoy.

You might realize that you connect better with people who share your intensity about specific topics, appreciate direct communication, or understand sensory sensitivities. These realizations can guide you toward friendships that feel more natural and sustainable.

You might also recognize that some friendships were built more on shared circumstances (work, neighborhood, children's activities) than on genuine compatibility, and that maintaining these connections requires more energy than they provide. **This recognition doesn't mean these relationships are worthless, but it might change how much time and energy you choose to invest in them.**

The goal isn't to eliminate all neurotypical friendships or only connect with other neurodivergent people, but to become more conscious about which relationships enhance your wellbeing versus which consistently require significant accommodation from you.

Authenticity and Connection Depth

Many people discover that their capacity for deep friendship actually increases as they become more authentic, even if their tolerance for superficial social connections decreases.

When you're not spending energy managing your presentation, you have more mental and emotional resources available for genuine connection, empathy, and care for others. Friends might notice that you're more present, more genuinely interested in their experiences, or more emotionally available when you're not simultaneously managing complex social performances.

However, this increased capacity for authentic connection often comes with decreased tolerance for surface-level social interaction that doesn't lead to meaningful connection. **You might find small talk more difficult or feel impatient with social activities that seem to serve no purpose beyond maintaining appearances.**

This shift can lead to confusion in friendships where much of the interaction has been based on light social contact rather than deep sharing. **Some friends might be ready and interested in deeper connection, while others might prefer to maintain the existing level of interaction.**

Identifying Energy Vampires vs. Supporters

Not all social connections affect your energy in the same way, and learning to distinguish between relationships that energize versus drain you is crucial for managing your social resources effectively. This distinction isn't about judging people as good or bad, but about recognizing compatibility patterns that affect your wellbeing.

Characteristics of Energy-Draining Relationships

Some relationships consistently leave you feeling depleted, anxious, or emotionally exhausted, even when the interactions seem positive on the surface. **These energy-draining patterns often reflect mismatches between your communication style and theirs, different values about time and energy, or dynamics that require extensive masking from you.**

Energy vampires might include people who:

- Consistently dominate conversations without reciprocal interest in your experiences
- Require extensive emotional support but aren't available when you need support
- Dismiss or minimize your needs and preferences
- Create drama or crisis situations that demand immediate attention and energy
- Expect you to accommodate their preferences while showing little flexibility about yours

The relationship might feel one-sided, with you consistently doing more of the emotional labor, accommodation, and energy investment to maintain the connection.

You might notice that you need significant recovery time after spending time with certain people, even when the interaction seemed pleasant. This emotional exhaustion often signals that the relationship requires more energy investment from you than it provides in return.**

Energy-draining friends might also be those who consistently expect you to participate in social activities that don't align with your sensory or energy needs, without showing willingness to accommodate your preferences. **They might pressure you to attend loud gatherings, criticize your need for quiet time, or make you feel guilty for having different social requirements.**

Recognizing Energy-Supporting Relationships

Supportive relationships leave you feeling understood, valued, and energized, even when the interactions involve serious topics or emotional sharing. These friends typically demonstrate curiosity about your authentic self and willingness to accommodate your neurological differences.

Energy supporters often:

- Show genuine interest in your thoughts, experiences, and perspectives

- Respect your communication style and don't try to change how you express yourself

- Accommodate your sensory and energy needs without making you feel burdensome

- Offer reciprocal emotional support and are available during your difficult times

- Appreciate your unique perspectives and contributions rather than trying to normalize you

These relationships often involve mutual accommodation – you both make adjustments to support each other's needs and preferences, creating a balanced dynamic rather than one-sided energy exchange.

You might notice that conversations with these friends flow naturally without requiring you to monitor and adjust your responses constantly. **You can discuss your genuine interests without feeling like you're being "too much," and you can express your needs directly without extensive justification.**

Time spent with supportive friends often feels restorative rather than depleting, even when you're discussing challenging topics or working through problems together.

The Gray Area: Conditional Support

Many friendships fall into a gray area where the person is supportive under certain conditions but becomes energy-draining when those conditions aren't met. **Understanding these conditional patterns helps you make conscious choices about how much energy to invest and when.**

A friend might be very supportive when you're functioning in ways they understand and appreciate, but become critical or distant when you need to express your neurodivergent traits more openly or when you're going through periods of higher support needs.

These friends might enjoy your company when you're masking effectively but express concern or confusion when you begin to unmask and be more authentic about your differences.

Conditional support isn't necessarily bad, but it's important to recognize the limitations so you can adjust your expectations and energy investment accordingly. You might choose to maintain these friendships at a level that works for both of you without expecting them to provide the deep understanding and acceptance you need during vulnerable times.

Making Strategic Friendship Choices

Once you can recognize energy patterns in your relationships, you can make more conscious choices about where to invest your social resources. This doesn't mean abandoning all relationships that require effort, but being strategic about the balance between energy investment and return.

You might choose to maintain some energy-draining relationships at a level that's sustainable for you – perhaps shorter visits, less frequent contact, or limiting the topics and depth of sharing. **The key is** making these choices consciously rather than automatically accommodating others' expectations.

Focus the majority of your social energy on relationships that provide mutual support, understanding, and genuine connection. These relationships are more likely to sustain you through difficult periods and celebrate your authentic self during good times.

Be willing to let some relationships naturally fade if they consistently require more energy than they provide and if the other person shows little interest in accommodating your needs or understanding your differences.

Building Neurodivergent Community Connections

Connecting with other neurodivergent people can provide a type of understanding and acceptance that's difficult to find in neurotypical-majority spaces. These communities offer the experience of being understood without extensive explanation and accepted without performance.

Online Neurodivergent Communities

The internet provides access to neurodivergent communities that might not be available in your local area. **Online spaces allow you to connect with others who share similar experiences, learn about resources and strategies, and participate in community without the sensory and social demands of in-person interaction.**

Social media platforms, forums, and chat groups dedicated to AuDHD, autism, ADHD, and general neurodivergence offer opportunities to share experiences, ask questions, and find support from people who understand your challenges and celebrate your differences.

Online communities can be particularly valuable for people who live in areas with limited neurodivergent resources or who have mobility, transportation, or scheduling constraints that make in-person participation difficult.

However, online communities also require energy management and boundary-setting. **Some online spaces might become overwhelming due to high activity levels, crisis-oriented discussions, or interpersonal conflicts.** Choose your online community participation strategically based on what serves your wellbeing rather than feeling obligated to engage with every available community.

Local Support Groups and Meetups

Many areas have in-person support groups, social meetups, or activity groups for neurodivergent adults. **These gatherings provide opportunities for face-to-face connection with others who understand your experiences without requiring extensive masking.**

Local neurodivergent groups might organize around specific activities (board games, hiking, crafts), support functions (newly diagnosed adults, workplace issues), or general social connection. The structured nature of many of these groups can make social interaction more comfortable for people who struggle with unstructured social situations.

Some groups are specifically for people with autism, ADHD, or AuDHD, while others welcome all neurodivergent individuals. **Consider which type of group might feel most comfortable and relevant for your specific experiences and needs.**

Be prepared that local groups might have varying levels of organization, consistency, and social dynamics. **It might take time to find groups that match your communication style, interests, and energy levels.**

Professional and Interest-Based Communities

Many professional fields and hobby communities have higher-than-average concentrations of neurodivergent individuals, making these spaces potentially more accepting of different communication styles, intense interests, and sensory needs.

Technology fields, academic environments, arts communities, gaming groups, and maker spaces often attract people with neurodivergent traits and may be more accommodating of different social and communication styles.

Joining communities based on your genuine interests rather than general social connection often leads to more satisfying relationships because you're connecting through shared passions rather than trying to create connection through small talk and surface-level interaction.

Professional associations, continuing education groups, volunteer organizations, and hobby clubs provide structured ways to meet like-minded people while engaging in activities that genuinely interest you.

Creating Your Own Community

If existing neurodivergent communities in your area don't meet your needs, consider starting your own group focused on your specific interests, age group, or support needs.

This might involve organizing informal meetups through social media, starting a book club for neurodivergent adults, creating activity groups around shared interests, or organizing support meetings for people with similar experiences.

Starting your own community allows you to set the tone, structure, and focus in ways that align with your communication preferences and energy needs.

Be prepared that organizing community activities requires ongoing effort and might not attract participants immediately. **Start small and build gradually based on interest and participation rather than trying to create a large group immediately.**

Maintaining Neurotypical Friendships

Understanding your AuDHD doesn't mean you need to abandon all friendships with neurotypical people. Many neurotypical individuals are capable of understanding, accommodating, and appreciating neurodivergent differences when provided with clear information and examples.

Education and Communication

Neurotypical friends who are genuinely interested in maintaining your friendship often respond positively to education about your AuDHD traits and needs. Clear communication about your differences can actually strengthen relationships by preventing misunderstandings and improving accommodation.

Help neurotypical friends understand that your social and sensory needs aren't preferences or choices, but neurological realities that affect your comfort and functioning. **Use specific examples from your shared experiences to illustrate how AuDHD traits affect your social participation.**

You might explain: "Remember how I always seem exhausted after big group gatherings? That's because I'm processing a lot more sensory and social information than most people, and it takes significant energy. It's not that I don't enjoy spending time with everyone – I just need recovery time afterward."

Be willing to suggest specific accommodations that would make social activities more comfortable for you, rather than just declining participation. This might involve meeting in quieter restaurants, providing advance notice about plans, or creating opportunities for one-on-one conversation within group settings.

Setting Realistic Expectations

Not all neurotypical friends will be able or willing to accommodate your neurodivergent needs fully, and adjusting your expectations can help preserve relationships that have other valuable qualities.

Some friends might be very accommodating about sensory needs but struggle to understand your communication style. Others might appreciate your directness but forget about your need for advance planning. **Focus on each friend's areas of strength and accommodation rather than expecting universal understanding.**

Be clear about which accommodations are essential versus which are preferences, so friends can prioritize their efforts effectively. A friend might not remember to provide detailed advance notice about social plans, but they might be willing to choose quieter venues when you remind them.

Accept that some neurotypical friendships might remain at a certain level of intimacy or involvement rather than becoming the deep, fully accommodating relationships you might prefer. **This limitation doesn't invalidate the friendship – it just defines its scope and role in your social life.**

Mutual Accommodation and Growth

Healthy neurotypical friendships involve mutual accommodation where both people adjust their behaviors and expectations to maintain the relationship. This reciprocity distinguishes supportive relationships from those where you're doing all the accommodating.

Your neurotypical friends might need to learn about sensory sensitivities, communication differences, and energy management, while you might need to be patient with their learning process and clearly communicate your needs rather than expecting them to guess.

Some neurotypical friends will surprise you with their capacity for understanding and growth, while others might plateau at a basic level of accommodation. Both outcomes are acceptable as long as the relationship feels balanced and mutually beneficial.

Be willing to appreciate and acknowledge when neurotypical friends make efforts to accommodate your needs, even if their accommodation isn't perfect. **Positive reinforcement encourages continued growth and shows that you value their efforts.**

Choosing Quality Over Quantity

Focus your energy on neurotypical friendships that demonstrate genuine care, flexibility, and interest in understanding your authentic self rather than trying to maintain all existing relationships at previous levels of involvement.

You might discover that some neurotypical friends become even closer when they can interact with your authentic self, while others drift away as you become less willing to mask extensively. **Both outcomes provide valuable information about relationship compatibility.**

The goal isn't to test or eliminate neurotypical friendships, but to invest your limited social energy in relationships that support your wellbeing and allow for genuine connection.

Social Energy Management

Understanding and managing your social energy is crucial for maintaining satisfying relationships without burning out or consistently overextending yourself. Social energy management for people with AuDHD often requires more planning and intentionality than neurotypical social patterns.

Understanding Your Social Battery

Your social battery operates differently than neurotypical patterns, and learning to recognize your energy levels, depletion signals, and recharge requirements helps you participate in social activities sustainably.

Notice how different types of social interaction affect your energy levels. **One-on-one conversations might feel energizing while group gatherings are draining, or structured activities might be more comfortable than unstructured social time.**

Pay attention to environmental factors that affect your social energy – noise levels, lighting, temperature, crowd density, and sensory stimulation all impact your capacity for social interaction.

Track your energy patterns over time to identify your optimal social activity levels, preferred spacing between social events, and most effective recovery strategies.

Learn to recognize early warning signs of social energy depletion before you reach complete exhaustion. **These might include increased sensory sensitivity, difficulty following conversations, desire to escape social situations, or decreased ability to filter your responses.**

Planning and Preparation Strategies

Strategic planning can help you participate in social activities more successfully by managing energy demands and creating conditions that support your comfort and engagement.

Request advance information about social events so you can prepare mentally and sensory-wise. **Knowing the location, duration, expected activities, and attendee list helps you plan appropriate coping strategies and set realistic expectations.**

Prepare exit strategies for social events so you can leave when your energy is depleted rather than pushing through to exhaustion. This might involve having your own transportation, setting time limits in advance, or creating acceptable reasons for early departure.

Consider your energy levels and recent social activity when accepting invitations. **Space social commitments to allow for recovery time between events rather than scheduling multiple social activities in quick succession.**

Bring tools that support your comfort during social activities – sunglasses for light sensitivity, noise-canceling headphones for overwhelming environments, fidget items for self-regulation, or snacks that help maintain your energy.

Recovery and Recharge Methods

Develop specific strategies for recharging your social energy after social activities, recognizing that this recovery time is necessary rather than optional for sustainable social participation.

Physical recovery might involve quiet environments with minimal sensory stimulation, comfortable clothing and temperatures, preferred foods and drinks, and physical positions that feel calming and restorative.

Mental recovery often includes engaging with special interests that provide positive stimulation, avoiding complex decision-making or problem-solving tasks, and having unstructured time without social or performance demands.

Emotional recovery might require processing your social experiences through journaling, talking with understanding friends, or simply allowing yourself to feel whatever emotions arose during social interaction without judgment.

The amount of recovery time needed varies based on the intensity and duration of social activity, your energy levels going into the activity, and your current overall stress and wellbeing status.

Communication About Energy Needs

Clear communication about your social energy needs helps friends and family understand your participation patterns and reduces the likelihood of misunderstandings or hurt feelings.

Explain that your need for social recovery time isn't about not enjoying their company or wanting to avoid relationships. **Help them understand that strategic energy management allows you to show up more authentically and consistently in your relationships.**

Be specific about what recharging looks like for you so others don't interpret your recovery activities as rejection or dismissal of your relationships.

You might say: "I had a wonderful time at the party, and I need some quiet time tomorrow to recharge my social battery. This helps me be more present and engaged when we spend time together later this week."

Set boundaries about contact during your recovery periods if necessary, explaining that you'll be more available and responsive after you've had time to recharge.

Friendship Audit Worksheet

Systematically evaluating your current friendships helps you make conscious decisions about where to invest your social energy and which relationships support your authentic self. This audit process isn't about judging people, but about recognizing compatibility patterns that affect your wellbeing.

Energy Impact Assessment

For each significant friendship, consider:

How do you typically feel during time spent with this person?

- Energized and engaged
- Comfortable and relaxed
- Neutral or mixed
- Drained but socially obligated
- Consistently exhausted or overwhelmed

How do you feel after spending time with this friend?

- Refreshed and satisfied
- Content and peaceful
- Tired but fulfilled
- Depleted and needing recovery
- Exhausted and dreading future contact

What types of activities do you typically do together?

- Activities that genuinely interest you both
- Activities that primarily interest them
- Activities that require significant accommodation from you
- Activities that consistently overwhelm your sensory system
- Activities that feel meaningful and connecting

How much masking do you need to do in this relationship?

- You can be completely authentic
- You mask occasionally for social smoothness
- You mask significantly but comfortably
- You mask extensively and it's exhausting
- You mask almost constantly when with this person

Communication and Support Patterns

How does communication flow in this relationship?

- Mutual sharing and reciprocal interest
- Mostly you listening to their experiences
- Mostly them accommodating your communication needs
- Frequent misunderstandings despite good intentions
- Consistent conflict or tension in conversations

How does this friend respond to your needs and boundaries?

- Accommodates readily and remembers your preferences
- Accommodates when reminded and shows genuine care
- Accommodates sometimes but often forgets
- Resists accommodation and argues about your needs
- Dismisses or invalidates your needs consistently

What support does this friendship provide during difficult times?

- Reliable emotional and practical support
- Good emotional support but limited practical help
- Support available but requires asking multiple times
- Support available only when convenient for them
- Limited or unreliable support during your difficulties

How available are you expected to be for their support needs?

- Reasonable requests that match your capacity
- Frequent requests that you can usually accommodate
- Demanding expectations that sometimes overwhelm you
- Crisis-oriented demands that disrupt your stability
- Constant emotional labor expectations

Compatibility and Growth Assessment

How well do your social and sensory needs align?

- Very compatible social preferences and energy levels
- Some differences but mutual accommodation works well
- Significant differences but friendship adapts around them
- Major incompatibilities that require extensive compromise
- Fundamental mismatches that create ongoing conflict

How has this friendship changed as you've become more authentic?

- Become deeper and more satisfying for both people
- Improved in some ways but challenging in others
- Remained stable with minor adjustments

- Become more strained or uncomfortable
- Deteriorated significantly or ended

What is this friend's capacity for learning and growth?

- Shows genuine curiosity and learns from education
- Willing to learn but requires patience and repetition
- Limited interest in learning but basic accommodation
- Resistant to new information about your differences
- Actively opposes or dismisses your authenticity

What unique value does this relationship provide?

- Deep understanding and mutual support
- Shared interests and intellectual connection
- Historical significance and emotional closeness
- Practical support and reliable presence
- Limited unique value beyond habit or obligation

Community Resource Directory

Building satisfying social connections often requires knowing where to look for compatible communities and activities. This directory provides starting points for finding neurodivergent-friendly social opportunities.

Online Communities and Resources

Social Media Platforms:

- Facebook groups for local neurodivergent communities
- Reddit communities for autism, ADHD, and AuDHD support
- Discord servers for neurodivergent social interaction

- Twitter/X hashtags and communities for neurodivergent experiences
- Instagram accounts focused on neurodivergent education and community

Specialized Platforms:

- Forums specifically designed for neurodivergent discussion
- Apps designed for neurodivergent social connection
- Virtual reality spaces with sensory-friendly options
- Online gaming communities with neurodivergent-friendly guilds
- Video chat groups organized around specific interests

Professional and Educational Resources:

- Webinars and online conferences about neurodivergence
- Online courses and workshops for neurodivergent adults
- Professional development groups for neurodivergent individuals
- Academic communities focused on neurodiversity research
- Training and certification programs with neurodivergent perspectives

Local Community Options

Support and Social Groups:

- Hospital or clinic-sponsored neurodivergent support groups
- Community center programs for neurodiverse adults
- Library programs and discussion groups
- Religious or spiritual communities with inclusion programs
- Volunteer organizations focused on neurodiversity advocacy

Activity-Based Communities:

- Board game cafes and gaming stores with regular meetups
- Maker spaces and craft workshops
- Hiking or outdoor activity groups
- Book clubs and literary societies
- Art classes and creative workshops
- Photography groups and camera clubs
- Technology meetups and coding groups

Professional and Educational Communities:

- Professional association local chapters
- Continuing education classes at community colleges
- Industry-specific networking groups
- Volunteer opportunities with organizations you support
- Adult education programs and workshops

Specialized Neurodivergent Organizations

National Organizations with Local Chapters:

- Autism self-advocacy organizations
- ADHD support and advocacy groups
- Neurodiversity advocacy organizations
- Disability rights organizations with neurodivergent focus
- Professional organizations for neurodivergent individuals

Regional and Local Specific Organizations:

- Local autism resource centers
- ADHD coaching and support organizations

- Neurodivergent social clubs and meetups
- Family and adult support programs
- Advocacy organizations focused on your geographic area

Online Organizations with Local Connections:
- National organizations that help connect local members
- Online communities with regional subgroups
- Professional networks with local chapters
- Interest-based organizations with geographic divisions
- Advocacy groups that organize local events

Social Battery Management System

Developing a systematic approach to managing your social energy helps you participate in relationships and community activities sustainably without consistently overextending yourself or avoiding social connection entirely.

Energy Monitoring and Tracking

Develop awareness of your current social energy levels by paying attention to physical, mental, and emotional indicators throughout the day and week.

Physical indicators might include:
- Energy levels and fatigue patterns
- Sensory sensitivity and tolerance levels
- Physical tension or relaxation states
- Sleep quality and appetite patterns
- Need for movement or stillness

Mental indicators often involve:
- Ability to focus and process information

- Decision-making capacity and mental clarity
- Memory function and organizational abilities
- Tolerance for complex or multi-step tasks
- Interest in learning or engaging with new information

Emotional indicators might include:

- Mood stability and emotional regulation
- Patience levels with frustration or confusion
- Enthusiasm for activities and relationships
- Capacity for empathy and emotional availability
- Response to social stimulation or interaction

Track these indicators over time to identify patterns in your social energy levels and optimal times for different types of social activities.

Pre-Social Planning Strategies

Prepare for social activities in ways that support your energy management and increase the likelihood of positive social experiences.

Environmental preparation:

- Research venue accessibility and sensory characteristics
- Plan transportation that minimizes stress and energy drain
- Identify quiet spaces or exit options at social locations
- Bring tools that support your comfort and regulation
- Prepare backup plans for overwhelming situations

Mental and emotional preparation:

- Set realistic expectations for social interaction quality
- Prepare conversation topics related to your genuine interests

- Practice responses to common social challenges you anticipate
- Plan energy conservation strategies during the social activity
- Identify specific goals or priorities for the social interaction

Physical preparation:

- Ensure adequate rest and nutrition before social activities
- Wear clothing that feels comfortable for expected activities
- Manage medications or supplements that affect energy levels
- Engage in regulating activities before social participation
- Address any physical needs that might become distracting

During-Social Energy Conservation

Use strategies during social activities to conserve energy and extend your capacity for meaningful participation.

Take strategic breaks:

- Step outside for quiet time when feeling overwhelmed
- Visit restrooms for brief solitude and sensory reset
- Take walking breaks if the activity permits movement
- Use transition times between activities for energy management
- Create opportunities for one-on-one conversation within group settings

Manage your participation level:

- Engage deeply in conversations that genuinely interest you
- Politely redirect or minimize participation in draining discussions

- Use your authentic interests as conversation topics when possible
- Be selective about which social activities you participate in fully
- Give yourself permission to be a quiet observer when needed

Monitor your energy levels:

- Check in with yourself regularly throughout social activities
- Notice early warning signs of energy depletion
- Adjust your participation based on current energy levels
- Communicate your needs to trusted friends when necessary
- Plan exit strategies before reaching complete exhaustion

Post-Social Recovery Protocols

Develop specific recovery routines that help restore your social energy after social activities, recognizing that this recovery is necessary for sustainable social participation.

Immediate recovery (first few hours):

- Engage in preferred sensory experiences that feel calming
- Avoid additional social demands or complex decision-making
- Allow yourself unstructured time without performance expectations
- Engage with special interests that provide positive stimulation
- Address physical needs like food, water, comfortable clothing

Extended recovery (following day or days):

- Maintain flexible schedules that accommodate varying energy levels

- Avoid scheduling additional social activities until energy returns
- Engage in activities that feel restorative rather than demanding
- Process social experiences through journaling or trusted conversation
- Practice self-compassion about any social missteps or exhaustion

Long-term energy management:
- Space social commitments to allow adequate recovery time
- Notice patterns in recovery needs after different social activities
- Adjust social participation levels based on overall life stress
- Build recovery time into your regular schedule rather than treating it as optional
- Communicate your recovery needs to friends and family members

Friendship Maintenance Strategies

Maintaining satisfying friendships when you have AuDHD often requires more intentional strategies than neurotypical friendship patterns because of differences in communication style, energy management, and social processing.

Communication Consistency

Develop sustainable communication patterns with friends that account for your energy levels and processing style rather than trying to match neurotypical communication expectations.

Be honest about your communication preferences: some people connect better through text messages, others through phone calls, and others through shared activities. **Match your communication style** to what feels authentic and sustainable rather than what seems socially expected.

Create systems for maintaining contact that don't rely solely on spontaneous communication. This might involve calendar reminders to check in with friends, regular scheduled calls or messages, or participation in ongoing group chats that don't require immediate responses.

Be direct about your communication needs: if you need time to process before responding to complex questions, or if you communicate more effectively through writing than speaking, share this information with understanding friends.

Set realistic expectations about response times and availability, helping friends understand that delayed responses don't indicate lack of care or interest in the relationship.

Mutual Accommodation Development

Work with friends to create relationship patterns that accommodate both of your needs rather than defaulting to neurotypical social expectations that might not work well for anyone involved.

Suggest social activities that align with both of your interests and energy levels rather than automatically participating in traditional social activities that might be draining for you.

Be willing to accommodate friends' needs while also communicating your own – this might mean choosing restaurants with quiet sections, meeting at times that work for both schedules, or finding activities that provide the right level of stimulation for both people.

Help friends understand which accommodations are most important for your comfort and participation, so they can prioritize their efforts effectively.

Express appreciation when friends make efforts to accommodate your needs, even if their accommodation isn't perfect. This positive reinforcement encourages continued growth and flexibility.

Conflict Resolution and Repair

Develop skills for addressing friendship conflicts in ways that account for your communication style and processing differences rather than using conventional conflict resolution approaches that might not fit your needs.

Be direct about concerns and misunderstandings rather than hoping friends will guess what's bothering you. **Many people with AuDHD communicate most effectively about problems through clear, specific statements rather than indirect hints.**

Ask for time to process when conflicts arise if you need space to think clearly about the situation before discussing solutions.

Focus on specific behaviors and situations rather than general character assessments when addressing friendship problems.

Be willing to explain how your neurodivergent traits might have contributed to misunderstandings without taking excessive blame for neurological differences that affect your communication or social processing.

Practice repair and reconnection after conflicts by acknowledging both people's experiences and working together to prevent similar problems in the future.

These insights pave the way for examining how to navigate professional environments and workplace challenges while maintaining authenticity and advocating for the accommodations that support your AuDHD success and wellbeing.

Chapter 9: Workplace Revolution

Thriving Professionally with AuDHD

Your career doesn't have to be a daily battle against your own brain. Yet for many people with AuDHD, work becomes an exhausting performance where they spend more energy managing their neurodivergent traits than actually contributing their skills and talents. **The traditional workplace wasn't designed with neurodivergent minds in mind, but that doesn't mean you can't find ways to thrive professionally while honoring your authentic self.**

Understanding your AuDHD changes everything about how you approach your career. **You can stop trying to force yourself into neurotypical work patterns that drain your energy and start building professional success around your actual strengths and needs.** This might mean advocating for accommodations in your current role, seeking out more compatible work environments, or even creating your own professional path through entrepreneurship.

The key insight is that your AuDHD traits aren't obstacles to overcome – they're part of your unique professional profile that can be leveraged for success when you understand how to work with them rather than against them.

Some of your challenges in traditional workplaces might actually point toward your greatest professional strengths. The intense focus that makes open office environments overwhelming might be perfect for deep analytical work. The direct communication style that feels awkward in small talk might be exactly what's needed in crisis management or technical problem-solving.

This doesn't mean professional life becomes effortless once you understand your AuDHD, but it means you can make strategic choices about where to invest your energy and how to structure your work life for sustainable success.

Disclosure Decisions and Strategies

Deciding whether, when, and how much to disclose about your AuDHD at work involves complex considerations that go far beyond simple honesty. Your livelihood, career advancement, and daily work experience can all be affected by disclosure decisions, making strategic thinking essential.

Assessing Workplace Culture and Safety

Before considering any level of disclosure, carefully evaluate your workplace culture's attitude toward differences, accommodations, and neurodiversity. **Some organizations genuinely support neurodivergent employees, while others may pay lip service to inclusion while maintaining environments that are hostile to anyone who doesn't fit traditional molds.**

Look for concrete evidence of inclusion rather than just official policies. **Does your organization actually employ and promote visibly neurodivergent individuals? Are accommodations viewed as reasonable supports or burdensome exceptions? How do managers and colleagues respond when people have different working styles or needs?**

Pay attention to how your workplace handles other types of differences and accommodations. **Organizations that are genuinely inclusive tend to be flexible and creative about supporting various employee needs, while those that merely claim to be inclusive often reveal their true attitudes through their responses to requests that require actual adaptation.**

Consider the power dynamics in your specific role and department. **Your immediate supervisor's attitude and flexibility matter more than company-wide policies if they control your day-to-day work experience and advancement opportunities.**

A software developer might work for a company with excellent diversity policies, but if their direct manager views accommodation requests as signs of weakness or lack of commitment, disclosure could negatively impact their career trajectory despite official protections.

Weighing Benefits and Risks

The potential benefits of workplace disclosure include access to formal accommodations, reduced energy spent on masking, increased authenticity in professional relationships, and protection under disability rights laws. These benefits can significantly improve your job satisfaction, performance, and long-term career sustainability.

However, disclosure also carries real risks in many workplaces. **These might include discrimination disguised as performance concerns, exclusion from advancement opportunities, increased scrutiny of your work, or colleagues treating you differently based on stereotypes about neurodivergence.**

The decision becomes more complex when you consider that some benefits of disclosure can be achieved without formal disclosure. You might be able to negotiate flexible work arrangements, request specific environmental modifications, or adjust your communication style without explicitly mentioning your AuDHD diagnosis.

Consider your specific accommodation needs and whether they require formal disclosure to implement effectively. **Some accommodations, like noise-canceling headphones or flexible scheduling, might be granted as general workplace wellness initiatives, while others, like modified performance evaluation criteria, might require formal disability disclosure.**

Timing Considerations

The timing of workplace disclosure can significantly affect how the information is received and what accommodations are possible. Consider both your own readiness and external circumstances that might influence your employer's response.

Disclosure during the hiring process allows you to assess employer attitudes and potentially negotiate accommodations before starting, but it also creates risk of hiring discrimination, despite legal protections that are often difficult to enforce in practice.

Disclosure after establishing yourself professionally means you have demonstrated competence and value before revealing your differences, but it might also mean you've been masking extensively and need significant changes to maintain your performance.

Crisis-driven disclosure – revealing your AuDHD because you're struggling or facing performance issues – often occurs when you have less negotiating power but might also create urgency around finding solutions.

Planned disclosure when you're performing well and want to optimize your work environment often provides the best foundation for positive accommodation discussions, but requires confidence in your workplace's inclusivity.

Levels of Disclosure

Not all workplace disclosure needs to be comprehensive. Consider what level of information serves your professional goals while protecting your privacy and energy.

Minimal disclosure might involve requesting specific accommodations without detailed explanation of their medical necessity. This approach works when your needs can be framed as productivity enhancements rather than disability accommodations.

Partial disclosure could involve sharing information about autism or ADHD individually rather than discussing the complexity of having both conditions. This strategy might feel more manageable and be easier for colleagues to understand.

Full disclosure includes comprehensive information about your AuDHD experience, how it affects your work, and what accommodations would be most helpful. This approach provides the most legal protection and potential for understanding, but also requires more energy and carries more risk.

Strategic disclosure varies the level of information shared with different people based on their need to know and capacity for understanding. You might share detailed information with HR and your direct supervisor while providing minimal information to colleagues.

Requesting Accommodations That Actually Help

The most legally protected accommodations aren't always the most practically helpful ones. Effective accommodation requests focus on specific changes that will genuinely improve your work performance and sustainability rather than generic accommodations that might be easier to approve but less impactful.

Understanding Your Specific Needs

Before requesting accommodations, develop clear understanding of which aspects of your work environment, schedule, or responsibilities create the biggest challenges for your AuDHD brain. **Generic accommodation requests are less likely to be approved and less likely to be helpful than specific requests tied to clear productivity benefits.**

Environmental accommodations might include lighting adjustments, noise reduction, workspace modifications, or flexibility about where you work. Consider which sensory factors most significantly affect your concentration, energy levels, and overall performance.

Schedule and timing accommodations could involve flexible start times, modified break schedules, advance notice of meetings, or adjustments to deadline structures. Think about your natural energy patterns and how traditional work schedules align with your optimal functioning times.

Communication accommodations might include receiving instructions in writing, having meeting agendas in advance, using email for complex discussions, or having modified evaluation processes that account for your communication style.

Task and responsibility accommodations could involve modified job duties, different approaches to meetings and presentations, alternative ways to demonstrate competence, or adjustments to multitasking expectations.

A marketing professional might identify that their biggest challenges are open office noise affecting their ability to write, last-minute meeting changes disrupting their planning systems, and expectations to participate in brainstorming sessions that feel overwhelming. Their accommodation requests would focus specifically on these areas rather than requesting generic "autism accommodations."

Framing Requests Strategically

Present accommodation requests in terms of productivity enhancement and business benefits rather than just personal need or legal entitlement. This framing helps employers understand accommodations as investments in your performance rather than burdens they're required to bear.

Connect your requests to specific work outcomes: "Having consistent lighting in my workspace helps me maintain focus for detailed analysis tasks, which improves the accuracy of my reports and reduces the time I need to spend on revisions."

Emphasize how accommodations enable your strengths: "When I have agenda items in advance, I can prepare thoughtful contributions to meetings rather than struggling to process information and generate responses simultaneously."

Address cost and implementation concerns proactively: "This accommodation would involve a one-time setup cost of approximately X and wouldn't require ongoing resources or changes to other employees' work environments."

Offer to trial accommodations to demonstrate their effectiveness: "I'd be happy to implement this change for a three-month trial period so we can evaluate its impact on my productivity and the team's functioning."

Documentation and Legal Protections

While you don't need to lead with legal language, understanding your rights helps you navigate accommodation discussions more confidently and provides recourse if employers resist reasonable requests.

The Americans with Disabilities Act (ADA) requires employers to provide reasonable accommodations that don't cause undue hardship to the business. **"Reasonable" accommodations are those that allow you to perform the essential functions of your job without fundamentally altering the nature of the position or creating excessive costs.**

Essential job functions are the core responsibilities that define your role, while non-essential functions might be modified or reassigned as accommodations. Understanding this distinction helps you focus accommodation requests on areas where flexibility is more legally required.

Interactive process requirements mean that employers must engage in good-faith dialogue about potential accommodations rather than simply denying requests. If initial requests are denied, employers should work with you to identify alternative solutions.

Documentation from healthcare providers can strengthen accommodation requests by establishing the medical basis for your needs, but this documentation should focus on functional limitations and necessary accommodations rather than detailed diagnostic information.

Common Effective Accommodations

Based on the experiences of many workers with AuDHD, certain types of accommodations tend to be both feasible for employers and genuinely helpful for neurodivergent employees.

Environmental modifications:

- Noise-reducing accommodations like private offices, noise-canceling headphones, or quieter workspace locations

- Lighting adjustments including desk lamps, different bulbs, or positioning away from fluorescent lighting

- Temperature control accommodations or flexibility to dress for personal comfort

- Workspace organization flexibility, including personal items that support focus and regulation

Schedule and structure accommodations:

- Flexible start/end times that align with natural energy patterns

- Modified break schedules that account for sensory and energy needs

- Advance notice of schedule changes and meeting requirements

- Reduced multitasking expectations or restructured responsibilities to support sustained focus

Communication accommodations:

- Written follow-up for verbal instructions and important information

- Meeting agendas and materials provided in advance

- Alternative meeting participation methods (written input, smaller group discussions)

- Modified feedback and evaluation processes that account for communication differences

Technology and tool accommodations:

- Specialized software for organization, time management, or task tracking

- Alternative input methods or assistive technology

- Flexibility to use personal tools and apps that support productivity
- Access to scheduling and reminder systems that match your planning style

Managing Paradoxical Needs at Work

Professional environments often require you to meet competing demands that can feel particularly challenging when you have both autism and ADHD traits. Learning to manage these paradoxical needs strategically can help you succeed in traditional workplaces while honoring your neurological differences.

Structure vs. Flexibility Balance

Your work might require both consistent processes (satisfying autism's need for predictability) and adaptive responses (engaging ADHD's need for variety). **Rather than trying to eliminate this tension, develop strategies that provide structure within flexibility or flexibility within structure.**

Create personal systems that provide consistent frameworks for handling variable demands. This might involve standard approaches to project planning that can be adapted to different types of assignments, or consistent daily routines that include flexible time blocks for unexpected tasks.

Use structure to support flexibility by developing decision-making frameworks, priority systems, and emergency protocols that help you respond adaptively to changing demands without losing your foundation of predictability.

A project manager might create standard project templates and communication protocols (structure) while building in buffer time and alternative approaches for handling unexpected changes (flexibility). This combination satisfies both the need for predictable processes and the ability to respond to dynamic project requirements.

Focus Depth vs. Breadth Requirements

Many jobs require both sustained focus on detailed tasks and broad awareness of multiple priorities and relationships. **Your AuDHD brain might naturally want to hyperfocus on interesting tasks while struggling to maintain attention on routine responsibilities that still need consistent management.**

Time-block your work to honor both needs: designate specific periods for deep focus work and separate times for broader awareness activities like email, planning, and relationship maintenance.

Use your intense focus periods strategically by scheduling your most complex or important tasks during times when you naturally hyperfocus, while handling routine tasks during periods when sustained attention is more difficult.

Create external systems to manage broad awareness needs when you're in hyperfocus mode, such as calendar reminders, task management apps, or accountability partnerships that help you transition between different types of work demands.

Social Engagement vs. Energy Management

Professional success often requires networking, collaboration, and relationship-building activities that can be energizing in small doses but exhausting when they become the primary focus of your work. **Balance social professional activities with work that allows for restoration and autonomous contribution.**

Schedule social professional activities strategically rather than accepting every networking opportunity or meeting invitation. Choose events and relationships that align with your professional goals and genuine interests.

Prepare for social professional demands by managing your energy proactively, planning recovery time, and developing authentic ways to engage that don't require extensive masking.

Find professional roles and projects that balance collaboration with independent work so you can contribute through both relationship-building and solo productivity.

An analyst might choose to attend industry conferences (high social engagement) but limit networking events to a few per year, focus on professional relationships that involve substantial technical discussion rather than pure socializing, and negotiate for project work that includes both collaborative planning phases and independent execution phases.

Innovation vs. Implementation

Your work might require both creative problem-solving (engaging ADHD novelty-seeking) and careful execution of established procedures (satisfying autism's need for thoroughness and accuracy). **These different types of thinking often require different energy and environmental conditions.**

Separate innovation and implementation phases of projects when possible, allowing yourself to engage fully with creative work during brainstorming phases and systematic work during execution phases.

Use your natural interest patterns to drive innovation work – you're likely to generate creative solutions for problems that genuinely engage your curiosity and concern.

Develop implementation systems that maintain your interest through gamification, progress tracking, or collaborative accountability rather than trying to power through routine execution tasks through willpower alone.

Seek roles and projects that match your natural balance of innovation and implementation interests rather than assuming you need to be equally strong in both areas.

Career Pivots and Finding AuDHD-Friendly Fields

Understanding your AuDHD might reveal that your current career path isn't aligned with your natural strengths and needs, or that your industry culture is fundamentally incompatible with authentic neurodivergent success. Strategic career pivoting can dramatically improve your professional satisfaction and long-term success.

Identifying Your Professional Strengths Pattern

Your AuDHD traits contribute to specific professional strengths that might not be valued in all industries but are highly valued in compatible fields. Identifying your strength pattern helps guide career decisions toward roles where your differences become advantages.

Pattern recognition and systems thinking often come naturally to AuDHD minds, making careers in data analysis, research, technology, and process improvement potentially rewarding.

Intense focus and attention to detail can be tremendous assets in fields requiring accuracy, thoroughness, and deep expertise, such as editing, quality assurance, technical writing, or specialized consulting.

Direct communication and problem-solving orientation might be valued in crisis management, technical support, project management, or roles requiring clear communication about complex topics.

Creative thinking and unconventional approaches can be assets in innovation-focused roles, entrepreneurship, artistic fields, or positions requiring novel solutions to persistent problems.

Strong sense of justice and authenticity might draw you toward advocacy, nonprofit work, education, or other mission-driven careers where your values align with your daily work.

A financial analyst might realize that their AuDHD traits make them excellent at pattern recognition in market data and detailed financial modeling, but terrible at the relationship management and sales aspects of their role. This insight might guide them toward more technical financial roles or specialized consulting rather than trying to force themselves into client-facing positions.

Evaluating Industry Cultures

Different industries have distinct cultures around communication, work relationships, sensory environments, and

expectations for conformity. Some industries are naturally more accommodating of neurodivergent traits, while others may be particularly challenging regardless of your specific role.

Technology and engineering fields often value direct communication, technical expertise, and focused work, though they can vary widely in their social and environmental demands.

Creative industries might appreciate unconventional thinking and intense passion for specific areas, but they often involve unpredictable schedules and high social demands.

Healthcare and education can be rewarding for people drawn to helping others, but they often involve high sensory demands, emotional labor, and strict institutional constraints.

Research and academia might suit people who thrive on deep investigation and specialized knowledge, but they often require extensive social networking and political navigation.

Finance and business can offer structured environments and clear metrics for success, but they often prioritize relationship-building and may have high-pressure, sensory-intensive cultures.

Government and nonprofit work might align with strong value systems and provide structured environments, but they often involve bureaucratic processes and political considerations that can be frustrating.

Making Strategic Career Transitions

Career transitions are rarely linear, especially when you're seeking environments that better accommodate neurodivergent traits. Strategic transitions involve building on your existing skills while gradually shifting toward more compatible environments and responsibilities.

Identify transferable skills that translate across industries, particularly those that align with your AuDHD strengths. Technical skills, analytical abilities, writing skills, and specialized knowledge often transfer well between fields.

Use your current role to develop skills and experiences that support your transition goals. Volunteer for projects that align with your target career direction, develop expertise in areas that interest you, and build a portfolio of work that demonstrates your capabilities.

Network strategically within your target field through professional associations, continuing education, volunteer work, or informational interviews that allow you to learn about industry culture and requirements.

Consider intermediate steps that move you closer to your goals without requiring dramatic immediate changes. This might involve internal transfers, consulting work, or part-time activities that build toward your ultimate career goals.

A teacher who realizes they're burned out by the social and sensory demands of classroom management might transition gradually by developing curriculum design skills, moving into educational technology roles, or specializing in one-on-one or small-group instruction rather than immediately leaving education entirely.

Building Authentic Professional Identity

As you develop your career around your AuDHD strengths, you can build a professional identity that integrates your neurodivergent traits rather than hiding them. This integration often leads to more sustainable success because you're working with your natural patterns rather than constantly fighting against them.

Develop expertise in areas that genuinely fascinate you rather than pursuing advancement opportunities that don't align with your authentic interests. Your natural intensity and focus are assets when applied to work you genuinely care about.

Build a reputation for specific strengths that come naturally to you, such as thorough analysis, creative problem-solving, or direct communication about difficult topics.

Seek leadership and advancement opportunities that leverage your authentic strengths rather than trying to develop neurotypical leadership skills that don't match your natural style.

Connect with others who appreciate your authentic professional contributions rather than trying to fit into professional cultures that require extensive masking and accommodation.

Entrepreneurship Considerations

For some people with AuDHD, entrepreneurship offers the ultimate opportunity to create work environments and structures that align with their neurological needs while capitalizing on their unique strengths. However, entrepreneurship also presents specific challenges that require careful consideration and strategic planning.

Advantages of Entrepreneurial Control

Creating your own business allows you complete control over your sensory environment, work schedule, communication patterns, and daily structure. You can design work processes that support your optimal functioning rather than adapting to systems created for neurotypical brains.

You can focus intensely on areas of genuine interest and expertise without having to balance unrelated responsibilities that drain your energy. Many successful neurodivergent entrepreneurs build businesses around their special interests or areas of deep knowledge.

Entrepreneurship can provide the variety and challenge that ADHD brains crave while allowing you to create predictable systems and routines that satisfy autism's need for structure.

You control disclosure decisions completely – you never have to navigate workplace accommodation discussions or worry about discrimination based on your neurological differences.

Direct communication and unconventional thinking – traits that can be challenging in traditional workplaces – often become entrepreneurial advantages when you're solving problems creatively and communicating directly with clients about their needs.

A software developer with AuDHD might start a consulting business focused on data analysis for nonprofits, allowing them to work in quiet environments, focus intensely on technical problems they find engaging, communicate directly with clients about project requirements, and structure their work schedule around their optimal energy patterns.

Entrepreneurial Challenges for AuDHD

However, entrepreneurship also requires skills and capabilities that can be challenging for people with AuDHD. Honest assessment of these challenges helps you develop strategies to address them or partner with others who complement your abilities.

Business development and marketing often require networking, relationship-building, and self-promotion that can be energy-intensive for people with social processing differences.

Financial management and business administration involve executive function skills like planning, organization, and attention to mundane details that might not align with your natural interests or strengths.

Uncertainty and variability in income, workload, and business demands can create stress if you need predictable structure and security to function optimally.

Multiple competing priorities and the need to handle various business functions simultaneously can be overwhelming if you prefer sustained focus on single tasks.

Client management and customer service require emotional labor and communication flexibility that might be draining if you prefer direct, task-focused interactions.

Strategic Approaches to Entrepreneurial Success

Successful neurodivergent entrepreneurs often develop specific strategies to leverage their strengths while addressing potential challenges through systems, partnerships, or business model choices.

Build businesses around your genuine expertise and interests rather than chasing market opportunities that don't engage your natural passion and knowledge.

Create systems and processes that support your executive function needs through scheduling tools, automated processes, clear workflows, and external accountability measures.

Consider partnerships or team structures that complement your abilities rather than trying to handle every aspect of business management independently.

Choose business models that align with your energy patterns and social preferences – some entrepreneurs thrive on client interaction, while others prefer product-based businesses with minimal direct customer service demands.

Plan for financial sustainability in ways that account for your specific needs for stability, predictable income, or flexibility around varying energy levels and productivity patterns.

Use your direct communication style as a business advantage by serving clients who value honesty, clarity, and straightforward problem-solving over relationship management and entertainment.

An entrepreneur with AuDHD might create a business model that involves developing technical training materials (leveraging deep expertise and focus abilities) while partnering with someone who handles sales and client relationship management, creating automated delivery systems that minimize ongoing customer service demands, and building financial reserves that accommodate natural fluctuations in productivity and energy.

Industry-Specific Accommodation Guides

Different industries have distinct cultures and practical constraints that affect which accommodations are feasible and how they're best implemented. Understanding industry-specific approaches helps you tailor accommodation requests to your professional context.

Technology and Engineering

Technology fields often have cultures that value productivity and results over conformity, making them potentially more receptive to accommodation requests that clearly support performance.

Common effective accommodations:

- Private offices or noise-reducing workspace modifications
- Flexible work schedules that align with peak productivity times
- Remote work options that eliminate commuting and office sensory challenges
- Modified meeting structures that include written agendas and follow-up documentation
- Task management tools and project tracking systems that support organization needs

Industry-specific strategies:

- Frame accommodations as productivity enhancements rather than disability needs
- Emphasize how accommodations support code quality, system reliability, or project efficiency
- Request technical tools and software that align with industry standards while meeting your specific needs
- Focus on deliverable-based performance measures rather than time-based attendance metrics

Healthcare and Human Services

Healthcare environments involve high sensory demands, emotional intensity, and strict regulatory requirements that can limit flexibility while creating significant accommodation needs.

Common effective accommodations:

- Modified break schedules that account for sensory recovery needs
- Written protocols and checklists that support attention to detail and reduce cognitive load
- Workspace modifications within regulatory constraints (lighting, organization, noise reduction)
- Communication accommodations that support accurate information processing
- Reduced multitasking expectations during complex procedures or documentation

Industry-specific strategies:

- Connect accommodation requests to patient safety and care quality
- Work within regulatory frameworks while advocating for reasonable modifications
- Emphasize how accommodations support accuracy, attention to detail, and sustained focus
- Consider specialized roles that match your strengths while meeting industry needs

Education and Training

Educational environments often involve high social demands, sensory challenges from classroom environments, and complex administrative requirements.

Common effective accommodations:

- Classroom environment modifications (lighting, noise control, organization systems)
- Modified teaching schedules that account for social energy management
- Written communication for complex administrative requirements
- Sensory break spaces and recovery time between high-demand activities
- Alternative approaches to professional development and collaboration requirements

Industry-specific strategies:

- Frame accommodations as supporting student learning outcomes
- Connect requests to educational effectiveness and professional sustainability
- Consider how accommodations might benefit student engagement and classroom management
- Work within educational regulations while advocating for reasonable modifications

Creative and Media Industries

Creative fields often appreciate unconventional thinking but may have unpredictable schedules, high social demands, and sensory-intensive work environments.

Common effective accommodations:

- Flexible work schedules that accommodate variable energy and creativity patterns
- Quiet spaces for focused creative work

- Modified collaboration approaches that support creative contribution
- Written communication options for complex project discussions
- Environmental controls that support sustained creative focus

Industry-specific strategies:

- Emphasize how accommodations support creative quality and innovative thinking
- Connect requests to project outcomes and creative deliverables
- Consider how sensory needs affect creative inspiration and productivity
- Frame accommodation needs as supporting artistic integrity and professional sustainability

Disclosure Scripts by Situation

Different workplace disclosure situations require different approaches and levels of detail. These scripts provide starting points that you can adapt to your specific circumstances and communication style.

Initial Job Interview Disclosure

"I want to be transparent about the fact that I'm neurodivergent – I have autism and ADHD traits that affect how I process information and work most effectively. This hasn't prevented me from being successful in my career, but I do work best in environments that allow for [specific needs like quiet workspaces, written communication, or flexible scheduling]. I'm happy to discuss any questions you have about how this affects my ability to do the job."

New Employee Disclosure

"I'd like to share some information about how I work most effectively. I have autism and ADHD, which means I process information differently and have some specific needs for optimal performance. I'm very committed to doing excellent work here, and there are some accommodations that help me contribute at my highest level. Can we schedule time to discuss how to set me up for success in this role?"

Established Employee Disclosure

"I've recently learned something about myself that explains some patterns you might have noticed in how I work. I have been diagnosed with autism and ADHD, which affects how I process information and manage various aspects of work. This doesn't change my commitment to my responsibilities, but it does help me understand why certain accommodations would significantly improve my performance and job satisfaction."

Performance Issues Disclosure

"I want to address the performance concerns we've discussed and share some context that might be helpful. I have autism and ADHD traits that affect how I function in certain work environments. I don't want to use this as an excuse, but I believe that with some specific accommodations, I can address these issues and perform at the level we both expect. Can we discuss some modifications that might help me succeed in this role?"

Project-Specific Disclosure

"For this project to be successful, I need to share some information about how I work most effectively. I have neurodivergent traits that mean I contribute best when I have [specific accommodations]. This has actually been an advantage in similar projects because [specific strengths]. Can we structure my participation in a way that leverages these strengths while accommodating my needs?"

Colleague/Team Disclosure

"I want to share something with the team that might help us work together more effectively. I'm neurodivergent – I have autism and ADHD – which means I communicate and process information differently than neurotypical people. This doesn't affect my commitment or capabilities, but it might help explain some differences you've noticed in how I approach work and interaction. I'm happy to answer any questions about how we can collaborate most effectively."

Accommodation Request Templates

Clear, specific accommodation requests are more likely to be approved and successfully implemented than vague or overly broad requests. These templates provide structure for different types of accommodation requests.

Environmental Accommodation Request

Subject: Workspace Accommodation Request to Support Performance

I am requesting a reasonable accommodation under the ADA to support my optimal job performance. I have [autism/ADHD/both] which affects my sensory processing and concentration abilities.

Specifically, I am requesting: [specific environmental modification]

This accommodation would help me by: [specific performance benefits]

The accommodation would involve: [specific implementation details and costs]

This modification would allow me to better perform the essential functions of my position, specifically: [list relevant job functions]

I am happy to discuss this request and explore alternative solutions that would meet both my needs and the organization's requirements. Thank you for considering this accommodation.

Schedule and Timing Accommodation Request

Subject: Schedule Modification Request for Optimal Performance

I am requesting a reasonable accommodation to modify my work schedule to better support my job performance. I have [condition] which affects my energy patterns and optimal functioning times.

I am requesting: [specific schedule modification]

This change would improve my performance by: [specific benefits]

I would maintain my full-time hours by: [explanation of how total hours would be preserved]

This modification would not affect my ability to collaborate with colleagues because: [explanation of coordination plans]

Essential job functions would continue to be met through: [specific performance commitments]

I believe this accommodation would benefit both my productivity and the team's overall effectiveness. I welcome the opportunity to discuss implementation details and address any concerns.

Communication Accommodation Request

Subject: Communication Accommodation Request

I am requesting reasonable accommodations for my communication and information processing needs. I have [condition] which affects how I process verbal information and express complex ideas.

I am requesting the following communication accommodations: [specific modifications]

These accommodations would improve my work performance by: [specific benefits]

Implementation would involve: [specific details about how accommodations would work]

These modifications would help me better fulfill essential job functions including: [list relevant functions]

I am committed to maintaining effective communication with colleagues and clients through these adapted methods. Please let me know if you need additional information or would like to discuss implementation details.

Technology and Tools Accommodation Request

Subject: Assistive Technology Accommodation Request

I am requesting reasonable accommodation in the form of assistive technology tools to support my job performance. My [condition] affects my [specific functional areas] and these tools would help me perform essential job functions more effectively.

Specifically, I am requesting: [list specific tools/software/equipment]

These tools would improve my performance by: [specific functional benefits]

The approximate cost would be: [cost estimate if known]

These accommodations would help me better perform: [essential job functions]

I have researched these tools and believe they represent cost-effective solutions that would significantly improve my productivity and job satisfaction. I welcome the opportunity to discuss implementation and demonstrate how these tools would benefit my work performance.

Career Assessment for AuDHD Strengths

Understanding your specific pattern of AuDHD strengths and challenges helps guide career decisions toward roles and environments where you can thrive professionally. This assessment framework helps identify your unique professional profile.

Cognitive Strengths Identification

Pattern Recognition and Systems Thinking:

- Do you naturally notice patterns in data, processes, or relationships that others miss?

- Are you drawn to understanding how complex systems work and interconnect?
- Do you enjoy identifying inefficiencies or improvements in existing processes?
- Are you skilled at troubleshooting problems by thinking through systematic causes and effects?

Deep Focus and Expertise Development:

- Do you naturally develop deep knowledge in areas that interest you?
- Can you sustain attention on complex tasks for extended periods when engaged?
- Do you prefer mastering specific domains rather than being a generalist?
- Are you known for thoroughness and accuracy in areas of expertise?

Creative Problem-Solving:

- Do you generate unconventional solutions to persistent problems?
- Are you comfortable with approaches that others might consider "outside the box"?
- Do you combine ideas from different domains in innovative ways?
- Are you energized by novel challenges that require creative thinking?

Detail Orientation and Quality Focus:

- Do you naturally notice errors, inconsistencies, or quality issues that others overlook?
- Are you motivated by accuracy and precision in your work?

- Do you prefer to complete tasks thoroughly rather than quickly?
- Are you skilled at quality assurance and verification processes?

Communication and Interpersonal Style Assessment

Direct Communication Preferences:

- Do you prefer straightforward, specific communication over indirect suggestions?
- Are you comfortable addressing problems and conflicts directly?
- Do you value honesty and authenticity in professional relationships?
- Do you find small talk and office politics draining or meaningless?

Teaching and Mentoring Abilities:

- Do you enjoy sharing knowledge about topics you understand well?
- Are you skilled at explaining complex concepts in clear, logical ways?
- Do you prefer one-on-one or small group interactions over large meetings?
- Are you patient with people who are genuinely trying to learn?

Collaborative Work Preferences:

- Do you work best in small, focused teams rather than large groups?
- Do you prefer structured collaboration with clear roles and expectations?

- Are you more comfortable with task-focused interaction than relationship-focused socializing?
- Do you contribute best when you can prepare for meetings and discussions in advance?

Work Environment and Structure Preferences

Sensory Environment Needs:

- Do you work best in quiet environments with minimal distractions?
- Are you sensitive to lighting, temperature, or noise in ways that affect your productivity?
- Do you prefer consistent sensory conditions rather than variable environments?
- Do you need control over your immediate workspace organization and setup?

Schedule and Routine Preferences:

- Do you function best with predictable schedules and advance notice of changes?
- Are there specific times of day when you're most productive or creative?
- Do you prefer sustained focus periods rather than frequent task-switching?
- Do you need flexibility to manage energy levels and sensory needs throughout the day?

Independence vs. Collaboration Balance:

- Do you prefer working autonomously with periodic check-ins rather than constant supervision?
- Are you comfortable with results-based evaluation rather than process monitoring?

- Do you need significant control over how you approach and complete tasks?
- Do you work well with minimal management as long as expectations are clear?

Values and Mission Alignment Assessment

Purpose and Meaning Requirements:

- Are you motivated by work that aligns with your personal values and interests?
- Do you need to understand how your work contributes to larger goals or outcomes?
- Are you drawn to roles that involve helping others or solving important problems?
- Do you prefer work that feels meaningful rather than just financially rewarding?

Justice and Fairness Orientation:

- Are you motivated by correcting inequities or improving systems?
- Do you notice when processes or policies create unfair outcomes?
- Are you comfortable advocating for changes that improve effectiveness or fairness?
- Do you prefer organizations with clear ethical standards and transparent practices?

Learning and Growth Opportunities:

- Are you energized by opportunities to develop new expertise?
- Do you prefer roles that involve ongoing learning rather than routine repetition?

- Are you motivated by challenges that require you to expand your knowledge and skills?

- Do you prefer organizations that support professional development and specialization?

These discoveries guide us toward understanding how to build sustainable daily life systems that support your AuDHD needs while managing the practical requirements of adult responsibilities, from organizing your living space to managing finances and healthcare.

Chapter 10: Daily Life Systems

Building Sustainable Routines

Creating daily life systems that work for your AuDHD brain is like designing a custom operating system – one that supports your natural patterns while helping you manage the practical demands of adult life. **The goal isn't to force yourself into neurotypical routines that constantly drain your energy, but to build flexible structures that provide stability while accommodating your changing needs.**

Most conventional productivity and organization advice assumes a neurotypical brain that can easily switch between tasks, maintain consistent motivation, and follow rigid systems indefinitely. **But your AuDHD brain needs something more sophisticated – systems that provide structure when you need predictability and flexibility when you need variety.**

The key insight is that sustainable daily life systems for AuDHD brains require what we might call "structured flexibility" – **frameworks that give you enough organization to reduce decision fatigue and executive function load while maintaining enough adaptability to accommodate your varying energy levels, interests, and circumstances.**

Think of it as creating a skeleton that supports your daily life without restricting your natural movement. **When your systems align with how your brain actually works, daily tasks become more manageable, leaving you with more energy for activities and relationships that bring meaning and joy to your life.**

This isn't about achieving perfect organization or maintaining flawless routines. **It's about creating life systems that support your wellbeing and effectiveness while being forgiving enough to accommodate the natural variations in how your AuDHD brain functions from day to day.**

Creating Flexible Structure (Routine with Escape Hatches)

Traditional routine advice often creates rigid systems that work well when life is predictable but fall apart when circumstances change or when your brain needs something different. Flexible structure provides the benefits of routine while maintaining the adaptability your AuDHD brain often requires.

Understanding Your Pattern Needs

Your autism traits likely crave some degree of predictability and routine, while your ADHD traits may need variety and spontaneity to maintain engagement. Rather than choosing between structure and flexibility, you can create systems that provide both simultaneously.

Identify which aspects of your day benefit most from consistency – these might include sleep schedules, meal timing, medication routines, or key transition points that help your brain shift between different types of activities.

Recognize which parts of your life need built-in flexibility – perhaps creative work time, social activities, or weekend schedules that can accommodate varying energy levels and interests.

A working parent might establish consistent morning routines that reduce decision-making and ensure essential tasks get completed, while keeping evening and weekend schedules more flexible to accommodate family needs and personal energy levels.

Consider your natural energy rhythms and attention patterns when designing routine elements. Your most structured routines should support rather than fight against your biological patterns.

Building Routine Frameworks

Instead of rigid schedules, create routine frameworks that provide structure while allowing for variation within established boundaries. These frameworks give your brain the predictability it needs while maintaining space for adaptation.

Time-based frameworks might involve consistent wake and sleep times with flexible activity scheduling in between, or regular meal times with variety in what you eat and where.

Activity-based frameworks could include consistent types of activities (morning self-care, focused work time, evening wind-down) with flexibility about the specific activities within each category.

Energy-based frameworks might involve matching different types of tasks to your natural energy patterns while allowing flexibility about which specific tasks you tackle when your energy is high or low.

Location-based frameworks could establish consistent spaces for different types of activities (work space, relaxation space, creative space) while allowing flexibility about how you use each space.

Creating Escape Hatches and Backup Plans

Escape hatches are built-in alternatives that allow you to maintain your overall routine structure even when specific elements aren't working on a particular day. These alternatives prevent the all-or-nothing thinking that can derail entire systems when one component fails.

For morning routines, escape hatches might include simplified versions for low-energy days, pre-prepared options that require minimal decision-making, or alternative sequences that achieve the same essential outcomes with different approaches.

For work productivity systems, backup plans could involve alternative work locations, different types of tasks for different mental states, or modified schedules that accommodate varying attention spans and energy levels.

For social and family commitments, escape hatches might include alternative ways to participate, modified versions of regular activities, or graceful ways to postpone or reschedule when you need recovery time.

A professional with AuDHD might have a detailed morning routine for high-energy days, a simplified version for moderate energy days, and a bare-minimum version for difficult days – all of which accomplish essential tasks while honoring their current capacity.

Seasonal and Cyclical Adjustments

Your needs for structure versus flexibility might change based on seasonal patterns, life circumstances, or natural cycles in your energy and attention. Building adjustment mechanisms into your systems prevents the need to completely rebuild routines when circumstances change.

Recognize your natural cycles – perhaps you need more structure during high-stress periods but more flexibility during stable times, or more routine during dark winter months but more spontaneity during energizing spring weather.

Plan for predictable life changes like work schedule shifts, family transitions, or seasonal mood changes by creating alternative versions of your core systems rather than trying to maintain identical routines year-round.

Build review and adjustment periods into your systems so you can consciously evaluate what's working and what needs modification rather than waiting until systems break down completely.

Document what works in different circumstances so you can return to effective approaches when similar situations arise again, rather than reinventing solutions each time.

Home Environment Optimization

Your living space significantly affects your daily functioning, energy levels, and overall wellbeing. Optimizing your home environment for your AuDHD needs can reduce daily stress, support better self-regulation, and create a foundation that makes everything else easier.

Sensory Environment Design

Your home should be a place where your sensory system can relax and regulate rather than constantly managing overwhelming input. This doesn't mean creating a sterile environment, but rather designing spaces that support your specific sensory preferences and needs.

Lighting considerations include having multiple lighting options for different activities and energy levels – bright light for focused tasks, soft light for relaxation, natural light exposure to support circadian rhythms, and the ability to control lighting levels throughout the day.

Sound management might involve identifying and reducing sources of distracting noise, creating quiet zones for rest and concentration, using sound masking or background noise that supports focus, and having noise-canceling options available when needed.

Visual organization often helps AuDHD brains function better – this might include reducing visual clutter in key areas, creating clear visual systems for organization, using color coding or labeling systems that match how your brain processes information, and designing visual calm in spaces where you rest and recharge.

Texture and tactile considerations include choosing fabrics, furniture, and materials that feel good to you, having sensory tools and comfort items easily accessible, and avoiding materials that create unpleasant tactile experiences in spaces where you spend significant time.

Organization Systems That Match Your Brain

Effective organization systems for AuDHD brains often look different from conventional organization advice because they need to account for both the systematic thinking of autism and the dynamic attention patterns of ADHD. The key is creating systems that reduce cognitive load while remaining flexible enough to evolve with your needs.

Visual organization systems work well for many AuDHD brains – this might include open storage where you can see items easily, clear containers for categorized items, visual reminder systems like calendars and task boards, and organization methods that don't rely solely on memory.

Category-based organization often aligns with autistic systematic thinking – grouping similar items together, creating logical storage systems, maintaining consistent locations for important items, and using categorization methods that make sense to your specific thinking patterns.

Accessibility-focused organization accommodates ADHD attention patterns – keeping frequently used items in easy-to-reach locations, reducing the steps required to put items away, creating systems that work even when you're in a hurry or distracted, and maintaining organization that supports rather than hinders daily functioning.

Flexibility within structure allows your organization systems to accommodate changing interests and needs – modular storage systems, adjustable organization tools, periodic review and reorganization opportunities, and systems that can grow and change with your life circumstances.

Creating Functional Zones

Rather than trying to maintain organization throughout your entire living space, creating functional zones allows you to focus your organizational energy where it matters most while accepting that some areas might be more flexible or chaotic. This approach prevents perfectionism from sabotaging your entire organization system.

Priority zones are areas where organization significantly impacts your daily functioning – perhaps your bedroom for sleep quality, kitchen for meal preparation, or work space for productivity. These areas deserve the most organizational attention and maintenance.

Transition zones help you shift between different activities or mental states – perhaps an entryway that helps you transition from public to private space, or a designated area for wind-down activities that signal the end of the work day.

Recovery zones are spaces specifically designed for rest, regulation, and recharging – areas with comfortable seating, preferred lighting, access to comforting items, and minimal organizational demands or visual stimulation.

Project zones accommodate your interests and creative activities without requiring constant setup and cleanup – spaces where you can leave projects partially completed, areas designed for specific types of activities, or flexible spaces that can be reconfigured based on current interests.

A person with AuDHD might maintain very organized systems in their bedroom and kitchen (essential for sleep and nutrition), have a flexible but functional home office space, create a cozy reading corner with soft lighting and comfortable seating, and dedicate a spare room or corner for creative projects that can remain set up between work sessions.

Managing Household Maintenance

Household maintenance tasks often challenge AuDHD brains because they're routine, ongoing, and don't align with natural interest patterns. Creating maintenance systems that work with rather than against your brain patterns makes these necessary tasks more manageable.

Batch similar tasks to take advantage of hyperfocus periods and reduce the mental overhead of task-switching – perhaps designating specific days for different types of cleaning, batching errands into single trips, or handling all administrative tasks during dedicated time blocks.

Use timers and external structure to support tasks that don't naturally engage your attention – setting specific time limits for cleaning tasks, using music or podcasts to make routine tasks more engaging, or creating accountability systems that provide external motivation.

Simplify maintenance systems to reduce the executive function load – choosing low-maintenance household items, reducing the number of products and tools needed for cleaning, creating simple daily maintenance routines rather than complex weekly systems, and accepting "good enough" rather than perfect maintenance standards.

Connect maintenance to values that do motivate you – perhaps maintaining organization to support creativity, keeping clean spaces for health and wellbeing, or creating welcoming environments for important relationships.

Task Management for Opposing Needs

Managing tasks effectively with AuDHD requires systems that can accommodate both the sustained focus of autism and the dynamic attention patterns of ADHD. Traditional task management approaches often assume consistent motivation and attention, which rarely matches AuDHD experiences.

Interest-Based Task Categorization

Rather than organizing tasks solely by priority or deadline, consider categorizing tasks based on the type of engagement they require from your brain. This approach helps you match tasks to your current mental state and energy levels.

High-interest tasks are those that naturally engage your curiosity or align with your special interests – these can often be scheduled for times when other tasks feel impossible but you still have mental energy for engaging activities.

Routine maintenance tasks require minimal mental engagement but benefit from consistent completion – these might be batched together, paired with more engaging activities, or scheduled for times when your brain needs less stimulating activities.

Complex analytical tasks require sustained focus and systematic thinking – these are often best scheduled for your peak attention periods and given adequate time without interruption.

Social or collaborative tasks require different types of energy and might need to be balanced with recovery time or scheduled when your social battery is charged.

Creative tasks might need flexibility in timing and approach, with systems that allow for both scheduled creative work and spontaneous creative opportunities.

Energy-State Task Matching

Your ability to complete different types of tasks varies based on your current energy, attention, and emotional state. Creating task lists organized by energy requirements helps you stay productive even when your capacity varies from day to day.

High-energy task lists might include complex projects, challenging problem-solving, difficult conversations, or tasks requiring sustained concentration – activities you tackle when you're feeling focused and motivated.

Medium-energy task lists could include routine work tasks, administrative responsibilities, planning activities, or tasks that require moderate but not intense attention.

Low-energy task lists might consist of simple organizational tasks, easy communication responses, routine self-care activities, or tasks that can be completed while listening to music or podcasts.

Recovery activity options provide alternatives when you need downtime but want to feel somewhat productive – perhaps light reading, gentle organizing, creative activities that don't require intense focus, or learning activities in areas of interest.

Emergency task protocols help you identify the absolute minimum requirements for difficult days when your capacity is significantly reduced – the essential tasks that maintain your basic functioning and most important responsibilities.

Flexible Deadline Management

Traditional deadline management assumes consistent productivity and motivation, but AuDHD brains often work in patterns of intense focus followed by periods of lower productivity. Flexible deadline systems accommodate these natural rhythms while still meeting external requirements.

Build buffer time into all deadlines to account for the natural variations in your productivity patterns – this might mean setting personal deadlines earlier than actual deadlines, breaking projects into phases with intermediate deadlines, or creating extra time for unexpected challenges or low-energy periods.

Create multiple completion stages for important projects so you can make progress even when you can't complete entire tasks – perhaps outline completion, first draft completion, revision completion, and final deadline stages.

Use hyperfocus periods strategically by having projects ready to tackle during periods of intense focus, maintaining lists of tasks that can be completed during hyperfocus sessions, and protecting hyperfocus time from interruptions when possible.

Develop task-switching systems that help you maintain progress on multiple projects without losing momentum – perhaps rotating between projects based on interest or energy levels, maintaining clear documentation about where you left off on paused projects, or creating systems that help you quickly re-engage with interrupted work.

Procrastination and Avoidance Management

Procrastination with AuDHD often reflects mismatches between task requirements and your current brain state rather than laziness or poor time management. Understanding the specific factors that contribute to task avoidance helps you develop more effective strategies.

Identify avoidance patterns – perhaps you avoid tasks that feel overwhelming, tasks without clear success criteria, tasks that require skills you feel insecure about, or tasks that interfere with more interesting activities.

Break down overwhelming tasks into smaller components that feel more manageable, create clear starting points that don't require significant mental energy, or identify which specific aspects of tasks feel most challenging.

Address emotional barriers to task completion – perhaps perfectionism that prevents starting imperfect work, anxiety about judgment or failure, or shame about past procrastination that creates additional avoidance.

Create accountability systems that support without creating additional pressure – perhaps body doubling with friends, gentle check-in systems, public commitment to deadlines, or reward systems that celebrate progress rather than just completion.

Use environmental changes to support task completion – changing work locations, removing distracting items, creating specific task-completion rituals, or pairing avoided tasks with preferred activities or environments.

Financial Planning with Executive dysfunction

Managing finances effectively when you have executive function differences requires systems that reduce cognitive load while providing the structure needed for long-term financial stability. Traditional financial advice often assumes capabilities that may not align with AuDHD patterns of attention and organization.

Simplifying Financial Systems

The more complex your financial systems, the more executive function resources they require to maintain. Simplifying your financial structure reduces the ongoing mental energy needed for money management while improving your ability to track and control your finances.

Minimize the number of accounts you need to actively manage – perhaps maintaining one checking account for daily expenses, one savings account for emergency funds, and one investment account for long-term goals rather than multiple accounts that require separate tracking and management.

Automate as many financial tasks as possible to reduce the number of decisions and actions required each month – automatic bill payments, automatic savings transfers, automatic investment contributions, and automatic transfers between accounts for different purposes.

Use simple budgeting categories that match how you actually think about money rather than complex systems that require detailed tracking – perhaps essential expenses, discretionary spending, and savings rather than numerous subcategories that become overwhelming to maintain.

Choose financial products that match your actual usage patterns rather than products that seem optimal in theory but require management approaches that don't align with your natural patterns.

A person with AuDHD might set up automatic transfers that allocate their paycheck into essential expenses, discretionary spending, and savings accounts, use automatic bill pay for all fixed expenses, and maintain simple tracking systems that don't require daily input or complex categorization.

Addressing Impulsivity and Spending Patterns

ADHD traits can contribute to impulsive spending decisions, while autism traits might lead to intense spending on special interests. Understanding these patterns helps you create financial systems that accommodate your natural tendencies while supporting your long-term goals.

Build spending delays into your financial systems – perhaps waiting periods before major purchases, separate accounts for discretionary spending that don't immediately affect essential expenses, or requiring multiple steps to access funds for non-essential purchases.

Plan for interest-based spending by budgeting specifically for your special interests rather than trying to eliminate this spending entirely – creating designated funds for books, technology, hobby supplies, or other areas of genuine interest.

Use environmental controls to support better spending decisions – removing saved payment information from websites, using cash for discretionary spending, avoiding shopping when you're experiencing strong emotions, or shopping with lists and predetermined spending limits.

Create positive spending systems that align with your values and long-term goals – perhaps automatic investments in areas you care about, planned purchases that support your hobbies and interests, or spending that enhances your quality of life in sustainable ways.

Emergency and Crisis Financial Planning

Executive function challenges can make financial crises more difficult to manage, making emergency planning particularly important for people with AuDHD. Creating systems in advance reduces the cognitive load during stressful periods when executive function may be compromised.

Maintain easily accessible emergency funds that don't require complex procedures to access – perhaps savings accounts that can be accessed quickly, emergency credit options that don't require application processes during crises, or small amounts of cash kept at home for immediate needs.

Document important financial information in easily accessible formats – lists of account numbers and contact information, instructions for accessing important accounts, information about automatic payments and financial obligations, and emergency contact information for financial institutions.

Create crisis protocols that reduce decision-making during emergencies – predetermined responses to different types of financial crises, simplified budgets for periods of reduced income, and clear priorities for essential versus non-essential expenses.

Build flexibility into your regular financial systems so they can accommodate periods of reduced income or increased expenses without completely breaking down – buffer funds that can handle income variations, spending plans that can be quickly reduced if necessary, and financial goals that can be temporarily paused without derailing long-term plans.

Health Management Strategies

Maintaining physical and mental health requires consistent attention to numerous details and ongoing self-advocacy – areas where executive function differences can create significant challenges. Effective health management systems reduce the cognitive load of healthcare while ensuring you receive appropriate care.

Medical Appointment and Information Management

Keeping track of multiple healthcare providers, appointments, medications, and medical information often overwhelms traditional organizational approaches. Creating centralized, simple systems helps ensure you receive appropriate care without becoming overwhelmed by healthcare management tasks.

Use centralized tracking systems for all medical information – perhaps a single digital app, physical notebook, or document that contains all healthcare providers' information, appointment history, medication lists, and important medical details.

Prepare standard information that you can provide consistently at medical appointments – current medication lists, symptom descriptions, questions you want to ask, and relevant medical history organized in formats that are easy to share with providers.

Create appointment preparation routines that help you make the most of medical visits – lists of current symptoms or concerns, questions about treatment options, information about how treatments are affecting your daily life, and any changes you've noticed since your last appointment.

Develop provider communication strategies that match your communication style – perhaps written questions, notes about important topics, or systems for following up on treatment recommendations and test results.

Plan for appointment recovery if medical visits tend to be draining – scheduling appointments at times when you can rest afterward, bringing comfort items or support people when appropriate, and having plans for managing any emotional or physical exhaustion that results from medical interactions.

Medication and Treatment Adherence

Managing medications and treatment recommendations consistently can be challenging when executive function affects memory, organization, and routine maintenance. Creating systems that support adherence without requiring perfect memory or organization improves health outcomes.

Use external memory supports for medication management – pill organizers, phone alarms, medication tracking apps, or other tools that don't rely on your memory to maintain consistency.

Connect medication timing to existing routine activities rather than trying to create entirely new habits – taking medications with meals, before brushing teeth, or with other established daily activities.

Plan for medication refills before you run out – automatic refill systems, calendar reminders, or other approaches that ensure continuity without requiring you to remember to request refills at the last minute.

Track treatment effectiveness in simple ways that help you communicate with providers about what's working – perhaps simple daily ratings, notes about significant changes, or tracking specific symptoms that treatments are meant to address.

Address adherence barriers directly rather than assuming willpower will solve consistency problems – perhaps difficulty swallowing pills, medication side effects, scheduling conflicts with dosing times, or cost issues that affect your ability to maintain treatment.

Preventive Care and Self-Advocacy

Preventive healthcare often requires you to schedule and attend appointments when you're feeling fine, advocate for your needs with busy healthcare providers, and maintain long-term awareness of your health patterns. These activities often challenge executive function but are crucial for long-term wellbeing.

Create preventive care schedules that don't rely on your memory – automatic appointment scheduling, annual reminders for routine care, or systems that help you maintain recommended screening and check-up schedules.

Develop self-advocacy skills that help you communicate effectively with healthcare providers – preparing questions in advance, bringing notes about your experiences, asking for clarification when you don't understand recommendations, and requesting accommodations that help you participate effectively in your healthcare.

Track long-term health patterns in ways that provide useful information without becoming overwhelming – perhaps simple symptom tracking, notes about medication effectiveness over time, or records of how different treatments affect your daily functioning.

Build healthcare teams that understand and support your neurodivergent needs – seeking providers who demonstrate patience and understanding, communicating your communication preferences and needs, and maintaining relationships with providers who support your authentic self-advocacy.

Connect health management to your broader values and goals rather than viewing it as isolated medical compliance – understanding how health affects your ability to pursue interests, maintain relationships, and achieve personal goals.

AuDHD-Specific Planning Templates

Generic planning systems often fail for AuDHD brains because they don't account for the complex interplay between structure needs and flexibility requirements. These specialized templates provide frameworks that honor both aspects of your neurological profile.

Daily Planning Template

Morning Reflection Questions:

- What is my current energy level (high/moderate/low/recovery mode)?
- What type of tasks align with my current mental state?
- What are my essential tasks for today (non-negotiable items)?
- What would make today feel successful regardless of how much I accomplish?
- What support or accommodations do I need today?

Daily Structure Framework:

- *Morning transition routine* (consistent elements that help you shift into daily activities)
- *Peak focus time* (1-3 hours scheduled for your most challenging or engaging tasks)
- *Routine task time* (batch processing of maintenance activities)
- *Flexible project time* (space for interest-driven work or creative activities)
- *Social/communication time* (scheduled time for emails, calls, social activities)
- *Recovery time* (built-in breaks and recharging activities)
- *Evening transition routine* (consistent elements that help you shift toward rest)

End-of-Day Review:

- What worked well about today's structure and activities?
- What felt challenging or energy-draining?
- What would I adjust for tomorrow based on today's experience?
- What am I grateful for or proud of about today?

Weekly Planning Template

Weekly Overview Process:

- Review upcoming appointments, deadlines, and commitments
- Assess your overall energy and capacity for the week
- Identify which days might be higher or lower demand
- Plan for necessary recovery time and self-care activities
- Balance routine tasks with engaging or creative activities

Weekly Categories:

- *Essential weekly tasks* (tasks that must happen but can be flexible about timing)
- *Interest-driven projects* (activities that align with current enthusiasms)
- *Social and relationship activities* (planned connection with others)
- *Health and self-care activities* (medical appointments, exercise, recovery time)
- *Maintenance and organization tasks* (household management, administrative tasks)

Weekly Flexibility Planning:

- Which activities have fixed timing versus flexible scheduling?

- What backup plans exist if energy or circumstances change?
- How will you handle unexpected changes or opportunities?
- What minimum requirements exist if this becomes a difficult week?

Project Planning Template

Project Initiation Questions:

- What genuinely interests me about this project?
- What specific outcomes define success for this project?
- What resources, skills, or support do I need?
- What are the realistic timeline and energy requirements?
- How does this project align with my broader goals and values?

Project Structure Framework:

- *Exploration phase* (research, brainstorming, initial planning)
- *Planning phase* (detailed organization, resource gathering, timeline creation)
- *Execution phases* (broken into manageable chunks with built-in flexibility)
- *Review phases* (regular assessment and adjustment opportunities)
- *Completion phase* (final steps, documentation, celebration)

Project Sustainability Elements:

- How will you maintain motivation throughout the project timeline?
- What will you do when hyperfocus energy naturally decreases?

- How will you handle obstacles or setbacks without abandoning the project?
- What support systems or accountability measures would be helpful?
- How will you celebrate progress and completion?

Sensory Home Audit Checklist

Creating a sensory-supportive home environment requires systematically evaluating how different aspects of your living space affect your nervous system. This audit helps identify modifications that could significantly improve your daily comfort and functioning.

Visual Environment Assessment

Lighting Evaluation:

- Are there multiple lighting options available in each room?
- Can you easily adjust lighting levels throughout the day?
- Do you have access to natural light during daytime hours?
- Are there any light sources that feel harsh, flickering, or uncomfortable?
- Do you have appropriate task lighting for detailed activities?
- Can you create dim, comfortable lighting for relaxation?

Visual Organization and Clutter:

- Do visual stimuli in your spaces feel calming or overwhelming?
- Are important items easy to locate visually?
- Do you have clear sight lines and uncluttered spaces where you need to focus?

- Are there areas with too much visual complexity or competing elements?
- Do your organizational systems support rather than hinder visual processing?

Color and Visual Design:

- Do the colors in your spaces feel energizing or calming as appropriate?
- Are there colors that consistently feel uncomfortable or distracting?
- Do you have visual elements that bring joy or interest without overwhelming?
- Are there spaces with visual simplicity when you need mental rest?

Auditory Environment Assessment

Noise Level and Quality:

- What are the typical noise levels in different areas of your home?
- Are there sources of unexpected or unpredictable sounds that feel jarring?
- Do you have access to quiet spaces when you need auditory rest?
- Are there background sounds that support focus or relaxation?
- Can you control noise levels in spaces where you need concentration?

Sound Masking and Management:

- Do you have tools available for managing overwhelming auditory input?

- Are there positive auditory elements (music, nature sounds) that support wellbeing?
- Can you easily modify sound environments based on current needs?
- Are there spaces designed specifically for auditory rest and recovery?

Tactile and Physical Comfort Assessment

Furniture and Surface Comfort:

- Do seating options provide appropriate support and comfort for extended use?
- Are there furniture options that match different comfort needs and activities?
- Do surfaces and materials feel pleasant to touch in spaces where you spend significant time?
- Are there uncomfortable textures that could be modified or avoided?

Temperature and Air Quality:

- Can you easily adjust temperature in different areas of your home?
- Are there options for different temperature preferences (warm and cool spaces)?
- Is air circulation adequate without being drafty or uncomfortable?
- Are there materials or products that affect air quality or scent in ways that bother you?

Physical Organization and Accessibility:

- Are frequently used items easily accessible without physical strain?

- Do organization systems support rather than hinder daily functioning?
- Are pathways clear and safe for different energy levels and attention states?
- Do physical arrangements support rather than compete with your natural movement patterns?

Budget Management Tools

Effective budget management for AuDHD brains requires systems that provide necessary oversight without creating overwhelming complexity or requiring unsustainable attention to detail. These tools balance financial awareness with cognitive accessibility.

Simplified Tracking Systems

Three-Category Budget System:

- *Essential expenses* (housing, utilities, groceries, transportation, minimum debt payments)
- *Discretionary spending* (entertainment, dining out, non-essential purchases, hobby expenses)
- *Future planning* (savings, investments, debt reduction beyond minimums, emergency funds)

Percentage-Based Budgeting:

- Allocate fixed percentages of income to different categories rather than tracking specific amounts
- Use automatic transfers to implement percentage allocations without ongoing management
- Adjust percentages periodically rather than tracking detailed expenses continuously
- Focus on overall balance rather than precise expense tracking

Priority-Based Spending Framework:

- Identify your top financial priorities (security, experiences, interests, relationships)
- Align spending decisions with these priorities rather than detailed budget categories
- Create simple decision-making criteria based on values rather than complex calculations
- Review and adjust priorities periodically rather than tracking daily spending decisions

Automation and Technology Tools

Automatic Financial Management:

- Set up automatic transfers for all fixed expenses and savings goals
- Use automatic bill payments to reduce monthly financial decision-making
- Create automatic investment contributions that don't require ongoing management
- Implement systems that separate discretionary spending from essential expenses automatically

Financial Tracking Apps and Tools:

- Choose apps that require minimal daily input but provide useful oversight
- Use apps that categorize expenses automatically rather than requiring manual entry
- Select tools that provide simple visual summaries rather than complex analytical reports
- Find apps that send helpful reminders without creating additional stress or obligation

Account Structure for Simplicity:

- Maintain separate accounts for different purposes to reduce complexity
- Use savings accounts that automatically accumulate funds for specific goals
- Keep checking accounts simple with minimal complexity or fees
- Consider tools that round up purchases and save the difference automatically

Financial Decision-Making Frameworks

Spending Decision Questions:

- Does this purchase align with my stated financial priorities?
- Will I still value this purchase in a week/month/year?
- Does this spending decision support or hinder my long-term goals?
- Am I making this purchase for genuine reasons or due to emotional impulses?
- Can I afford this purchase without affecting essential expenses or savings goals?

Major Purchase Planning:

- Build waiting periods into major purchase decisions
- Research purchases during interest phases but delay buying decisions
- Create specific savings goals for anticipated major purchases
- Consider the total cost of ownership rather than just initial purchase prices

- Plan for the ongoing costs and maintenance of significant purchases

Crisis Financial Decision-Making:

- Identify which expenses are truly essential versus those that feel important
- Create predetermined criteria for financial emergency responses
- Maintain emergency funds that are accessible but separate from daily spending
- Have clear protocols for handling unexpected income changes or major expenses
- Know where to seek financial advice and support during difficult periods

Medication and Appointment Tracking

Managing healthcare information effectively reduces stress around medical care while ensuring you receive appropriate treatment and can advocate effectively for your needs. These systems organize health information without creating overwhelming complexity.

Centralized Health Information System

Essential Health Information Documentation:

- Current medication list with dosages, prescribing doctors, and pharmacy information
- Healthcare provider contact information including primary care, specialists, and emergency contacts
- Insurance information and coverage details
- Medical history summary including significant diagnoses, surgeries, and treatments

- Current symptoms or concerns that affect daily functioning
- Emergency medical information and emergency contacts

Medication Management System:

- Use pill organizers or electronic reminders for daily medication consistency
- Maintain current medication lists in easily accessible formats
- Track medication effectiveness and side effects in simple formats
- Plan for prescription refills before running out of medications
- Document questions about medications to discuss with providers
- Keep emergency medication information easily accessible

Appointment Management and Preparation

Appointment Scheduling and Tracking:

- Use calendar systems that provide adequate reminders and preparation time
- Schedule appointments at times that work with your energy patterns and other commitments
- Plan for appointment preparation and recovery time
- Maintain records of appointment outcomes and follow-up requirements
- Track which providers and appointment types work best for your needs

Medical Appointment Preparation:

- Prepare standard information packets with current medications, symptoms, and questions

- Write down questions and concerns before appointments to ensure important topics are addressed
- Bring comfort items or support people to appointments when helpful
- Plan for appointment recovery time if medical visits tend to be draining
- Prepare systems for following up on treatment recommendations and test results

Health Pattern Tracking

Simple Symptom and Wellness Tracking:

- Use simple rating systems rather than detailed symptom logs
- Track patterns that affect daily functioning rather than every health variation
- Note correlations between treatments, lifestyle factors, and wellbeing
- Document information that helps with medical communication and treatment decisions
- Focus on trends and patterns rather than daily variations

Treatment Effectiveness Monitoring:

- Track how different treatments affect your ability to function in work, relationships, and daily activities
- Note both positive effects and side effects of treatments
- Document questions about treatment effectiveness to discuss with providers
- Maintain records of what has been tried and what has been most helpful
- Track long-term patterns rather than daily fluctuations in treatment response

With this foundation established for managing daily life systems, you can build the skills and knowledge needed to navigate crisis situations and advocate effectively for your needs during challenging periods when your usual systems might be disrupted or when you need additional support.

Chapter 11: Crisis Management and Self-Advocacy

Navigating Challenges with Confidence

Life inevitably includes periods of crisis, challenge, and unexpected disruption – times when your usual coping strategies might feel insufficient and your AuDHD traits can become more pronounced due to stress. Rather than hoping you never encounter difficulties, building crisis management skills and self-advocacy capabilities creates resilience that helps you navigate challenges while maintaining your wellbeing and authenticity.

Understanding how to recognize early warning signs, manage acute stress responses, and advocate for your needs during difficult periods transforms crises from devastating disruptions into manageable challenges. **This doesn't mean crises become easy, but it means you have tools and strategies that help you maintain some control and direction even during your most difficult moments.**

Crisis management for people with AuDHD often looks different from conventional advice because your nervous system processes stress differently, your communication needs may be more specific, and your recovery requirements might not match typical expectations. **Effective crisis management honors these differences while building practical skills for handling emergencies, advocating with healthcare providers, understanding your legal rights, and creating support systems that function when you need them most.**

The goal isn't to prevent all difficult experiences – that's neither possible nor necessarily beneficial for growth and resilience. Instead, the goal is developing competence and confidence in your ability to navigate challenges while maintaining your authentic self and accessing appropriate support.

This preparation pays dividends not just during major crises, but during smaller daily challenges where self-advocacy skills and stress management techniques help you address problems before they become overwhelming.

Recognizing and Preventing Burnout

AuDHD burnout often develops gradually through the accumulation of stressors, masking demands, and energy depletion that can be difficult to recognize until it becomes severe. Learning to identify early warning signs allows you to take preventive action before reaching complete exhaustion.

Understanding AuDHD Burnout Patterns

Burnout in people with AuDHD typically involves the intersection of sensory overwhelm, social exhaustion, executive function breakdown, and the energy depletion that comes from constantly managing neurological differences in environments not designed for neurodivergent brains.

Unlike typical work burnout that might resolve with vacation time, AuDHD burnout often requires comprehensive attention to multiple areas of life because it stems from systemic mismatches between your neurological needs and environmental demands rather than just work-related stress.

The progression often follows predictable patterns: initial increased masking and accommodation to manage environmental demands, gradual depletion of energy reserves, decreased ability to maintain usual coping strategies, increased sensory sensitivity and emotional reactivity, and finally breakdown of essential functioning in multiple life areas.

Early stage indicators might include needing more recovery time after social activities, increased irritability with sensory stimuli that usually don't bother you, difficulty maintaining organization systems that typically work well, or increased effort required to complete routine tasks.

Middle stage warning signs often involve decreased tolerance for change or unpredictability, withdrawal from social activities that previously felt manageable, increased reliance on comfort items or familiar routines, difficulty making decisions that typically feel straightforward, or noticeable changes in sleep, appetite, or emotional regulation.

Late stage burnout typically includes inability to maintain masking behaviors, significant changes in functioning at work or in relationships, complete overwhelm from normal daily demands, physical symptoms like chronic fatigue or frequent illness, or feeling disconnected from interests and activities that typically provide meaning and satisfaction.

Environmental and Social Stressors

Many factors that contribute to AuDHD burnout are environmental rather than personal, making it important to identify external stressors that can be modified rather than assuming burnout reflects personal failure or inadequate coping skills.

Workplace stressors might include open office environments, frequent meetings without recovery time, unclear expectations or frequent changes in priorities, social demands that require extensive masking, or lack of accommodations for sensory sensitivities and executive function differences.

Social and relationship stressors often involve extended periods of masking in social situations, relationships that require significant emotional labor without reciprocal support, family or friend dynamics that invalidate your needs, or social obligations that consistently drain more energy than they provide.

Environmental stressors include living situations with poor sensory conditions, commuting in overwhelming environments, lack of quiet spaces for recovery, exposure to unpredictable noise or lighting, or inability to control your physical environment adequately.

Life transition stressors such as job changes, moving, relationship changes, health issues, or family transitions can be particularly challenging because they disrupt established coping systems while requiring additional energy for adaptation.

A working professional might experience burnout from the combination of an open office environment, increased meeting demands, family stress, and seasonal changes that affect their energy levels – each individual stressor might be manageable, but the combination exceeds their adaptive capacity.

Personal Warning Systems

Developing personalized early warning systems helps you recognize burnout risk before reaching crisis levels. These systems should account for your specific patterns and be simple enough to maintain even when your executive function is compromised.

Physical warning signs might include changes in sleep patterns, appetite changes, increased frequency of headaches or physical tension, changes in coordination or increased clumsiness, or increased susceptibility to illness or infection.

Emotional warning signs often involve increased irritability or emotional reactivity, feeling overwhelmed by decisions that typically feel manageable, increased anxiety about routine activities, feelings of disconnection from activities you usually enjoy, or increased negative self-talk or self-criticism.

Cognitive warning signs include difficulty concentrating on tasks that normally engage your attention, increased forgetfulness or disorganization, difficulty processing information that's usually straightforward, increased mental fatigue, or feeling like your thinking is slower or less clear than usual.

Behavioral warning signs might involve withdrawing from social activities, abandoning self-care routines, increased reliance on comfort objects or activities, changes in eating or exercise patterns, or decreased ability to maintain your usual productivity levels.

Social warning signs often include increased conflict in relationships, withdrawal from people who usually provide support, increased masking effort required for typical interactions, feeling misunderstood or disconnected from others, or difficulty maintaining your usual social energy and engagement.

Prevention Strategies

Preventing burnout requires proactive management of energy expenditure and recovery rather than waiting until exhaustion occurs. These strategies work best when implemented consistently rather than only during high-stress periods.

Energy budgeting involves consciously tracking and managing your energy expenditure across different life domains – work responsibilities, social commitments, household management, and self-care activities – to ensure you're not consistently spending more energy than you have available.

Recovery scheduling means building regular restoration time into your routine rather than trying to power through periods of high demand. This might include daily quiet time, weekly recovery periods, seasonal adjustments to your activity levels, or planned breaks after high-stress events.

Environmental modifications focus on reducing unnecessary stressors in your daily environment – improving lighting and noise conditions at home and work, creating sensory-friendly spaces, organizing your physical environment to reduce cognitive load, or negotiating accommodations that support your optimal functioning.

Boundary management involves setting and maintaining limits on energy-draining activities and relationships – saying no to commitments that don't align with your priorities, limiting time spent in overwhelming environments, communicating your needs clearly to others, or ending relationships that consistently require more energy than they provide.

Support system development includes building relationships and resources that provide genuine support during difficult periods rather than additional demands – identifying people who understand your neurodivergent needs, connecting with professional resources, creating emergency support plans, or joining communities that provide understanding and practical assistance.

Meltdown and Shutdown Management

Meltdowns and shutdowns are neurological responses to overwhelming stress or stimulation, not behavioral choices or character flaws. Understanding these responses and developing management strategies helps you navigate these experiences with self-compassion while minimizing their impact on your daily life.

Understanding Neurological Responses

Meltdowns typically involve externalized responses to overwhelming stimulation or stress – they might include crying, verbal outbursts, physical restlessness or agitation, difficulty communicating clearly, or behaviors that help discharge overwhelming internal pressure.

Shutdowns usually involve internalized responses where your nervous system essentially goes offline to protect itself from further stimulation – they might include inability to speak or communicate, extreme fatigue, disconnection from your environment, difficulty processing information, or feeling like you're observing your experience from a distance.

Both responses are protective mechanisms that your nervous system uses when input or demands exceed your processing capacity. They're not signs of weakness, immaturity, or poor coping skills – they're natural responses to neurological overwhelm that require understanding and management rather than judgment or suppression.

Triggers often involve sensory overload from environments with too much noise, light, or activity; social overwhelm from extended masking or complex interpersonal situations; cognitive overwhelm from excessive demands or complex problem-solving; emotional overwhelm from intense situations or accumulated stress; or physical overwhelm from pain, illness, or fatigue.

The progression typically involves gradual increase in stress or stimulation, decreased ability to use usual coping strategies, warning signs that overwhelm is approaching, the meltdown or shutdown response itself, and a recovery period during which normal functioning gradually returns.

Early Intervention Strategies

Recognizing the early warning signs allows you to take action before reaching complete overwhelm. These interventions are most effective when practiced during calm periods and used proactively rather than waiting until crisis occurs.

Environmental modifications might include leaving overwhelming situations when possible, reducing sensory input through lighting changes or noise reduction, finding quiet spaces for temporary recovery, removing yourself from social demands, or creating physical comfort through preferred textures, temperatures, or positions.

Sensory regulation techniques could involve using noise-canceling headphones or earplugs, seeking preferred sensory input like soft textures or gentle pressure, engaging in movement that helps regulation like walking or stretching, using visual tools like sunglasses or eye masks, or accessing preferred scents or tastes that promote calm.

Communication strategies include using predetermined signals to request help or space, having scripts for requesting accommodations, preparing written explanations for common situations, asking trusted people to help communicate your needs when you can't do so yourself, or using alternative communication methods when verbal communication becomes difficult.

Cognitive regulation approaches might involve using grounding techniques that connect you to your immediate environment, engaging in simple counting or naming exercises, focusing on breathing or other physical sensations, using familiar scripts or phrases that provide comfort, or accessing special interests that provide positive focus and regulation.

During-Crisis Management

When you're in the midst of a meltdown or shutdown, your capacity for complex problem-solving and communication is significantly reduced. Crisis management strategies need to be simple, accessible, and practiced in advance.

For meltdowns, focus on safety first – ensure you're in a safe environment where you won't harm yourself or others, remove yourself from triggering stimulation when possible, use physical techniques that help discharge energy safely like squeezing objects or controlled movement, and avoid making important decisions or having complex conversations until the intensity decreases.

For shutdowns, prioritize basic care and recovery – find safe, quiet spaces where you can rest without demands, minimize sensory input and social interaction, use comfort items or familiar objects that provide security, allow time for your system to reset without pressure to function normally, and avoid forcing communication or activity until you naturally begin to reengage.

For both responses, remember that this experience is temporary and will pass, avoid judging yourself for having these responses, use whatever communication methods feel accessible even if they're not your usual approaches, accept help from trusted people who understand your needs, and plan for recovery time after the crisis passes.

Recovery and Reflection

Recovery from meltdowns and shutdowns typically takes longer than the crisis itself and requires gentle, patient attention to your nervous system's need to restore equilibrium.

Physical recovery might involve extra sleep, preferred foods and drinks, comfortable clothing and environments, gentle movement or stretching, and avoiding additional stressors while your system stabilizes.

Emotional recovery often includes processing the experience without judgment, reconnecting with your sense of safety and stability, engaging with comforting activities or interests, seeking understanding and support from trusted people, and practicing self-compassion about having these responses.

Cognitive recovery involves gradual re-engagement with normal activities, avoiding complex decision-making until you feel clearer, returning to familiar routines that provide structure and predictability, and slowly increasing your activity level based on your energy and capacity.

Learning and adjustment includes reflecting on triggers and warning signs, identifying which interventions were most helpful, adjusting your environment or routine to reduce future risk, communicating with important people about your needs and experiences, and building these insights into your ongoing self-care and crisis management plans.

A person might notice that their meltdowns often occur after several days of high social demands combined with poor sleep, leading them to build more recovery time into their schedule after social events and prioritize sleep hygiene during busy periods.

Healthcare Self-Advocacy

Navigating healthcare systems while neurodivergent often requires specific self-advocacy skills because many healthcare providers have limited understanding of how AuDHD affects health, communication, and treatment needs. Effective self-advocacy ensures you receive appropriate care while maintaining your dignity and authenticity.

Preparing for Medical Appointments

Preparation significantly improves the quality of your healthcare interactions because it allows you to communicate effectively even when medical appointments feel overwhelming or when providers have limited time for complex discussions.

Document your current concerns in writing before appointments, including specific symptoms, changes you've noticed, questions about treatments, and how health issues affect your daily functioning. Written documentation helps ensure important topics are addressed even if you become overwhelmed during the appointment.

Prepare your medical history in easily accessible formats, including current medications with dosages, previous treatments and their effectiveness, important medical events, family medical history, and any accommodations or communication preferences that help you participate in healthcare effectively.

Identify your communication needs and plan to communicate them to providers – perhaps you process information better when it's written down, need extra time to formulate responses to complex questions, prefer direct communication rather than euphemisms, or work better with providers who explain procedures and expectations clearly.

Plan for appointment logistics that support your optimal functioning – scheduling appointments at times when your energy and focus are typically best, arranging transportation that minimizes stress, bringing comfort items or support people when appropriate, and planning for recovery time after appointments if medical interactions tend to be draining.

Prepare questions and concerns in writing rather than relying on memory during appointments, prioritizing your most important concerns in case time runs short, including questions about treatment options and side effects, and preparing follow-up questions about implementing recommendations in your daily life.

Communicating with Healthcare Providers

Effective communication with healthcare providers often requires adapting your natural communication style while still advocating clearly for your needs. The goal is conveying important information accurately while building cooperative relationships with your healthcare team.

Be direct and specific about your symptoms and concerns rather than expecting providers to infer problems from indirect communication – describe specific symptoms, their frequency and impact, what makes them better or worse, and how they affect your daily functioning and quality of life.

Provide context about how your AuDHD affects your health experiences – perhaps sensory sensitivities affect your response to treatments, executive function differences affect medication adherence, communication differences affect how you report symptoms, or social processing differences affect your comfort with certain procedures.

Ask for clarification when you don't understand treatment recommendations, medication instructions, test procedures, or follow-up requirements – request written information when possible, ask providers to repeat important information, request explanations of medical terms or concepts, and make sure you understand next steps before leaving appointments.

Advocate for accommodations that help you participate effectively in your healthcare – perhaps written summaries of appointment discussions, advance information about procedures, modified communication approaches, environmental accommodations during appointments, or alternative ways to access healthcare services.

Express your preferences about treatment approaches, communication styles, and healthcare delivery methods – discuss which treatment options align with your lifestyle and values, communicate about provider communication approaches that work best for you, and express preferences about appointment scheduling, follow-up methods, and healthcare coordination.

Addressing Healthcare Discrimination and Misunderstanding

Unfortunately, some healthcare providers may have limited understanding of neurodivergence or may hold biases that affect

the quality of care they provide. Recognizing and addressing these issues protects your health while advocating for better treatment.

Recognize discrimination that might be disguised as medical judgment – providers who dismiss your symptoms as anxiety or attention-seeking, who make treatment decisions based on assumptions about your intelligence or competence, who refuse to provide accommodations that don't require significant resources, or who treat you disrespectfully because of your communication style or needs.

Document concerning interactions including dates, provider names, specific statements or behaviors that felt discriminatory, witnesses if available, and impacts on your healthcare experience – this documentation can be useful for addressing problems with supervisors, insurance companies, or regulatory bodies.

Seek second opinions when you feel your concerns aren't being addressed appropriately, when treatment recommendations don't align with your understanding of your condition, when providers seem dismissive of your symptoms or needs, or when you don't feel heard or respected in healthcare interactions.

Know your rights regarding healthcare access, accommodation, and treatment – the right to receive care without discrimination, the right to request accommodations that don't create undue burden, the right to have your medical information kept confidential, the right to participate in treatment decisions, and the right to seek alternative providers if your needs aren't being met.

Build healthcare teams that include providers who demonstrate understanding and respect for neurodivergent patients – seek recommendations from other neurodivergent individuals, look for providers with specific training or experience in neurodiversity, prioritize providers who demonstrate patience and flexibility, and maintain relationships with providers who support your self-advocacy.

Managing Complex Healthcare Needs

People with AuDHD often have complex healthcare needs that require coordination between multiple providers and ongoing self-advocacy to ensure appropriate care. Effective management prevents important issues from being overlooked while avoiding healthcare system overwhelm.

Coordinate between providers by maintaining comprehensive medical records, sharing relevant information between different specialists, ensuring all providers know about your medications and treatments, communicating about how different treatments affect each other, and advocating for healthcare team communication when you have multiple conditions or providers.

Track treatment effectiveness in ways that provide useful information for healthcare decisions – noting how treatments affect your daily functioning, energy levels, cognitive clarity, emotional regulation, and overall quality of life rather than just specific symptoms.

Plan for healthcare emergencies by maintaining easily accessible medical information, ensuring important people know about your medical conditions and communication needs, having emergency contact information readily available, preparing emergency care instructions that account for your neurodivergent needs, and planning for healthcare advocacy if you're unable to communicate effectively during emergencies.

Address medication management challenges that might arise from executive function differences, sensory sensitivities to medications, interactions between different treatments, or difficulties with traditional medication schedules – work with providers to find approaches that align with your actual lifestyle and capabilities rather than ideal medication management scenarios.

Legal Rights and Protections

Understanding your legal rights and protections provides foundation for effective self-advocacy in various life domains

while ensuring you can access appropriate accommodations and support. Knowledge of these rights empowers you to advocate confidently for fair treatment and necessary accommodations.

Disability Rights and Accommodations

The Americans with Disabilities Act (ADA) provides comprehensive protections against discrimination and ensures access to reasonable accommodations in employment, public accommodations, and other areas of life. Understanding these protections helps you advocate effectively for your needs.

Employment protections include the right to reasonable accommodations that don't create undue hardship for employers, protection from discrimination in hiring and promotion decisions, the right to keep medical information confidential, protection from harassment based on disability status, and the right to perform essential job functions with or without accommodations.

Public accommodations must be accessible and provide reasonable modifications to policies and procedures – this includes retail establishments, restaurants, entertainment venues, healthcare facilities, and educational institutions making modifications that allow equal access to services.

Educational rights include accommodations in academic settings, modifications to testing and evaluation procedures, access to appropriate educational services, and protection from discrimination in educational environments.

Housing rights involve reasonable accommodations in housing policies and procedures, modification of rules that prevent equal enjoyment of housing, and protection from discrimination in housing rental and purchase decisions.

Transportation rights include access to public transportation, reasonable modifications to transportation policies, and accommodations that ensure equal access to transportation services.

Workplace Rights and Accommodations

Employment law provides specific protections and accommodation rights that can significantly improve your work experience when you understand how to access and implement these protections effectively.

Reasonable accommodations might include modifications to work schedules, changes to the work environment, modifications to equipment or technology, changes to job duties or responsibilities, and alternative ways to perform essential job functions.

Interactive process requirements mean that employers must engage in good-faith dialogue about potential accommodations, consider various accommodation options, provide accommodations that are effective for the employee's needs, and document accommodation discussions and decisions.

Documentation requirements for accommodations typically involve medical documentation of functional limitations, specific accommodation needs, and how proposed accommodations would address work-related challenges – but employers cannot require extensive medical information beyond what's necessary to establish accommodation needs.

Protection from retaliation means that employers cannot take negative action against employees who request accommodations, file discrimination complaints, or exercise their rights under disability protection laws.

Confidentiality protections ensure that medical information shared for accommodation purposes must be kept confidential and only shared with supervisors or colleagues who need to know for accommodation implementation.

Healthcare Rights and Patient Advocacy

Healthcare patients have specific rights regarding treatment, information access, and accommodation that are particularly

important for neurodivergent individuals who may need modified communication or care approaches.

Informed consent rights include receiving information about treatments in ways you can understand, having adequate time to consider treatment options, asking questions about risks and benefits, and having your treatment preferences respected when medically appropriate.

Communication accommodations in healthcare settings might include receiving information in writing, having extra time for appointments, bringing support people to appointments, using alternative communication methods when needed, or having procedures explained in detail before they occur.

Access to medical records allows you to obtain copies of your medical information, review test results and treatment notes, share information between providers, and correct errors in medical records when they occur.

Privacy protections ensure that your medical information cannot be shared without your consent except in specific legally required circumstances, and that you have control over who has access to your medical information and how it's used.

Quality care rights include receiving care that meets professional standards, being treated with respect and dignity, having your cultural and personal preferences considered in treatment planning, and receiving care that's appropriate for your individual needs and circumstances.

Self-Advocacy in Legal and Administrative Contexts

Legal and administrative processes often require specific self-advocacy skills and knowledge to ensure fair treatment and appropriate outcomes. These skills are particularly important when dealing with disability benefits, educational accommodations, or discrimination complaints.

Documentation and record-keeping form the foundation of effective legal self-advocacy – maintaining records of important conversations and decisions, documenting discriminatory treatment or accommodation failures, keeping copies of all relevant paperwork and correspondence, and organizing information in ways that support your advocacy efforts.

Understanding processes and procedures helps you navigate complex systems more effectively – knowing deadlines and requirements for various legal processes, understanding your rights and obligations in different situations, knowing when you need professional assistance, and understanding how to access resources and support.

Communication in formal settings often requires adapting your natural communication style while still advocating effectively – presenting information clearly and concisely, focusing on facts and specific examples, maintaining professional tone while being assertive about your needs, and following up in writing when appropriate.

Accessing professional support when needed ensures you receive appropriate assistance with complex legal issues – knowing when to consult attorneys, understanding what different types of legal professionals can provide, accessing low-cost or free legal services when available, and preparing effectively for consultations with legal professionals.

Emergency Planning

Emergency planning for people with AuDHD requires considering how crisis situations might affect your communication, decision-making, and functioning abilities while ensuring you have access to appropriate support and accommodations. Effective planning reduces stress during emergencies while ensuring your needs are understood and met.

Personal Emergency Preparedness

Personal emergencies might include medical crises, mental health crises, sudden changes in living situations, job loss, or other situations that disrupt your normal routines and support systems. Planning for these possibilities helps you maintain some control and direction during overwhelming situations.

Emergency contact systems should include multiple people who understand your neurodivergent needs, clear information about who to contact for different types of emergencies, backup contacts in case primary contacts are unavailable, and instructions for emergency contacts about your communication preferences and needs.

Medical emergency planning involves maintaining easily accessible medical information, ensuring emergency responders understand your communication needs and medical conditions, having plans for healthcare advocacy if you can't communicate effectively, preparing medication and treatment information for emergency situations, and planning for recovery and follow-up care after medical emergencies.

Financial emergency planning includes maintaining accessible emergency funds, having important financial information organized and accessible, planning for income disruption or increased expenses, knowing how to access emergency financial assistance, and having systems for managing finances if your executive function is compromised during crises.

Communication emergency planning involves preparing alternative communication methods for when verbal communication is difficult, having written information about your needs and preferences, identifying people who can help communicate your needs, preparing scripts or templates for common emergency communication needs, and ensuring important people understand your communication patterns during stress.

Crisis Response Plans

Crisis response plans provide structured approaches to handling different types of emergencies while accounting for how stress

might affect your typical functioning abilities. These plans work best when they're simple, accessible, and practiced in advance.

Mental health crisis planning includes recognizing warning signs of mental health emergencies, having clear steps for accessing immediate support, identifying trusted people who can provide assistance, preparing information for mental health professionals, and planning for recovery and follow-up care after mental health crises.

Medical crisis planning involves having medical information easily accessible, ensuring emergency contacts understand your medical needs and communication preferences, planning for medical advocacy during emergencies, preparing for hospital stays or medical procedures, and organizing follow-up care and recovery support.

Safety crisis planning includes identifying safe spaces and safe people during emergencies, having plans for removing yourself from dangerous situations, preparing emergency supplies and resources, knowing how to access emergency services, and planning for temporary housing or support if needed.

Workplace crisis planning might involve having backup systems for essential work responsibilities, preparing colleagues or supervisors for your potential absence, organizing important work information for accessibility during crises, planning for accommodation needs during crisis recovery, and knowing your rights regarding medical leave and workplace support.

Support System Activation

During emergencies, your usual support systems may need to be activated quickly and effectively. Planning these systems in advance ensures help is available when you need it most.

Primary support network should include people who understand your neurodivergent needs, can provide different types of assistance (practical, emotional, advocacy), are available at different times and under different circumstances, understand your communication preferences during stress, and can coordinate with each other when multiple types of support are needed.

Professional support resources might include healthcare providers who understand your needs, mental health professionals with neurodivergent expertise, legal or advocacy professionals, financial advisors or assistance programs, and case managers or coordinators who can help navigate complex systems during crises.

Community support resources could involve disability advocacy organizations, neurodivergent community groups, religious or spiritual communities, neighborhood or local support networks, and online communities that can provide understanding and assistance during difficult periods.

Emergency service interaction planning includes preparing information for emergency responders about your communication needs, having plans for requesting accommodations during emergency service interactions, identifying advocates who can help communicate with emergency services, preparing for law enforcement interactions that account for your neurodivergent traits, and planning for hospital or institutional stays that might be required during emergencies.

Burnout Early Warning System

Developing a personalized early warning system helps you recognize burnout risk before reaching crisis levels, allowing for preventive intervention rather than crisis management. This system should be simple enough to maintain consistently and sensitive enough to detect problems before they become severe.

Physical Monitoring Indicators

Physical changes often provide the earliest and most reliable indicators of increasing burnout risk because they reflect your nervous system's response to accumulated stress before you might consciously recognize emotional or cognitive changes.

Sleep pattern changes might include difficulty falling asleep despite being exhausted, waking up frequently during the night, sleeping much more or much less than usual, feeling unrefreshed after sleep, or changes in dreams or nighttime anxiety that affect sleep quality.

Energy and fatigue patterns often shift before other symptoms become obvious – feeling tired despite adequate rest, needing more caffeine or stimulation to function normally, physical exhaustion that doesn't improve with rest, decreased stamina for activities that typically feel manageable, or feeling like you're "running on empty" frequently.

Physical health changes might involve increased susceptibility to minor illnesses, headaches or muscle tension that don't have clear causes, changes in appetite or digestion, increased clumsiness or coordination difficulties, or physical symptoms that seem related to stress but don't have clear medical explanations.

Sensory sensitivity changes often intensify during burnout development – sounds, lights, or textures that typically don't bother you becoming overwhelming, needing to avoid sensory input that you usually enjoy, feeling overwhelmed in environments that typically feel comfortable, or requiring more sensory accommodations than usual.

Emotional and Cognitive Indicators

Changes in emotional regulation and cognitive functioning often signal that your stress management systems are becoming overwhelmed and that intervention is needed to prevent further deterioration.

Emotional regulation changes might include increased irritability over minor issues, feeling overwhelmed by decisions that typically feel straightforward, crying more easily or feeling emotionally numb, increased anxiety about routine activities, or feeling disconnected from activities and relationships that usually provide satisfaction.

Cognitive function changes often involve difficulty concentrating on tasks that normally engage your attention, increased forgetfulness or disorganization, feeling like your thinking is slower or less clear, difficulty processing information that's usually straightforward, or mental fatigue that doesn't improve with rest.

Motivation and interest changes might include decreased enthusiasm for activities you typically enjoy, difficulty starting tasks that usually feel manageable, feeling like nothing sounds appealing or worthwhile, procrastinating more than usual, or losing interest in hobbies or special interests that typically provide energy and satisfaction.

Self-perception changes often involve increased negative self-talk or self-criticism, feeling like you're failing at things you typically handle well, questioning your abilities or competence, feeling like you're letting others down, or losing confidence in your problem-solving abilities.

Behavioral Pattern Changes

Changes in your typical behavior patterns often reflect your brain's attempts to manage increasing stress through adaptation strategies that may provide short-term relief but indicate underlying system strain.

Social behavior changes might include withdrawing from people who usually provide support, avoiding social activities you typically enjoy, feeling like social interactions require more energy than usual, increased conflict in relationships, or feeling misunderstood or disconnected from others.

Work and productivity changes often involve decreased efficiency on tasks that typically feel manageable, avoiding challenging projects or responsibilities, increased procrastination, difficulty meeting deadlines that typically aren't problematic, or feeling overwhelmed by work demands that usually feel reasonable.

Self-care behavior changes might include abandoning routines that typically support your wellbeing, eating more or less than usual, avoiding exercise or movement that typically helps you feel better, neglecting medical appointments or health maintenance, or increased reliance on substances or behaviors that provide temporary relief.

Coping behavior changes often involve increased use of avoidance strategies, relying more heavily on comfort items or familiar activities, becoming more rigid about routines or preferences, avoiding new experiences or challenges, or using coping strategies that worked in the past but may not be effective for current stressors.

Intervention and Response Protocols

Once early warning signs are recognized, having predetermined intervention strategies helps you respond effectively before burnout becomes severe. These protocols should be tailored to your specific patterns and resources.

Immediate intervention strategies might include reducing optional commitments and activities, increasing rest and recovery time, modifying your environment to reduce sensory stress, reaching out for support from trusted people, or implementing stress management techniques that have been effective for you in the past.

Short-term adjustment strategies could involve modifying work responsibilities or schedules, rearranging social commitments, seeking professional support, adjusting medication or health management approaches, or making environmental changes that reduce daily stress.

Long-term prevention strategies might include examining lifestyle patterns that contribute to burnout risk, developing better boundary-setting skills, building stronger support systems, addressing ongoing stressors that contribute to vulnerability, or making structural changes to your life that support sustainable functioning.

Professional support activation involves knowing when to seek additional help from healthcare providers, mental health professionals, workplace accommodation specialists, or other professionals who understand neurodivergent needs and can provide appropriate support during challenging periods.

With these concepts in place, you have developed a comprehensive toolkit for understanding and managing your AuDHD experience – from initial discovery and identity integration through practical daily management and crisis preparedness. This foundation supports ongoing growth, authenticity, and resilience as you continue building a life that honors your neurodivergent brain while achieving your personal goals and values.

Chapter 12: Understanding Your Loved One's Discovery

A Partner's Guide to AuDHD

When someone you love discovers they're AuDHD, it can feel like meeting them all over again. The person sitting across from you at breakfast is the same person you've shared your life with, yet suddenly there's this new lens through which everything makes sense - their quirks, their struggles, their unique way of moving through the world. This discovery isn't just theirs; it becomes part of your shared journey.

Many partners describe feeling a mix of relief ("Finally, we have answers") and uncertainty ("What does this mean for us?"). These feelings are completely normal. You're not just supporting someone through a medical diagnosis - you're both navigating a fundamental shift in understanding that touches every aspect of your relationship.

The person you love hasn't changed overnight. What's changed is the framework for understanding behaviors, needs, and experiences that may have puzzled both of you for years. That rigid adherence to routines? The way they shut down in crowded spaces? How they hyper-focus on projects for hours but struggle to remember appointments? These aren't character flaws or things they choose to do - they're expressions of a beautifully complex brain that operates differently.

What Late Diagnosis Means for Relationships

Late diagnosis brings unique challenges to relationships that couples rarely anticipate. Unlike other medical conditions that have clear treatment paths, AuDHD discovery often means rewriting the story of your relationship - understanding past conflicts through a new lens and adjusting expectations for the future.

The Reframe Period typically lasts several months to a few years. During this time, both partners are essentially learning a new language for their relationship. Conversations that once led to frustration ("Why can't you just...") transform into collaborative problem-solving ("How can we make this work for both of us?"). This period requires patience from both people as you figure out what accommodation looks like in your daily life.

Common relationship impacts include changes in communication patterns, household management, social obligations, and intimacy. The partner who seemed "high-maintenance" about textures and sounds now makes perfect sense. The one who appeared "antisocial" at parties wasn't being difficult - they were managing overwhelming sensory input while trying to navigate complex social dynamics.

Financial dynamics often shift as well. AuDHD individuals may need specific accommodations - noise-canceling headphones, particular foods, modified work schedules, or therapy. These aren't luxuries; they're accessibility needs that help your partner function at their best. Understanding this distinction helps prevent resentment from building around expenses that might seem unnecessary to neurotypical thinking.

Decision-making processes frequently require adjustment. AuDHD brains often need more processing time for big decisions, detailed information about changes, and the ability to research thoroughly before committing. What might seem like indecisiveness is actually a different cognitive process that, when respected, leads to more thoughtful outcomes.

The social calendar becomes a collaboration rather than an assumption. Your partner might need advance notice for social events, the ability to leave early, or quiet recovery time afterward. This isn't antisocial behavior - it's energy management. Learning to plan together around these needs strengthens your partnership rather than limiting it.

Supporting Without Enabling and Managing Emotions

The line between support and enabling can feel impossibly thin when your partner is navigating AuDHD discovery. Support helps someone build skills and confidence; enabling removes their agency and creates dependence. Understanding this distinction protects both your well-being and your partner's growth.

Healthy support looks like problem-solving together rather than solving for them. When your partner struggles with executive function tasks like paying bills or organizing schedules, offer to create systems together rather than simply taking over the tasks. You might sit down monthly to review finances together, set up automated payments, or establish shared calendars with reminders.

Ask questions that empower: "What would make this easier for you?" "How can we set this up so it works with your brain?" "What support would be most helpful?" These questions respect their autonomy while offering your partnership.

Enabling behaviors to avoid include constantly reminding them about responsibilities they can learn to manage independently, making excuses for them in social situations without their input, or assuming they can't handle certain tasks. Enabling often comes from love and a desire to help, but it can inadvertently communicate that you don't believe in their capabilities.

Managing your own emotions throughout this process requires intentional attention. It's normal to feel grief for the relationship dynamic you thought you had, uncertainty about the future, or even frustration with the learning curve. These feelings don't make you a bad partner - they make you human.

Create space for your emotions without making them your partner's responsibility. This might mean talking with friends who understand, joining a support group for partners of neurodivergent individuals, or working with a therapist who can help you process this transition.

Patience with the process serves both of you. Your partner is learning about their brain while simultaneously trying to unmask years of camouflaging behaviors. This internal work is exhausting and can temporarily make them seem more sensitive, withdrawn, or emotionally volatile. Understanding this as part of the discovery process rather than a permanent change helps you maintain perspective.

Celebrating small victories builds momentum for both of you. When your partner successfully advocates for their needs at work, manages a social situation without overwhelm, or establishes a helpful routine, acknowledge these achievements. Growth happens in increments, and recognizing progress keeps you both motivated.

Setting boundaries protects your relationship's sustainability. You can be supportive while maintaining your own needs and limits. This might mean agreeing on how many social events to attend per month, establishing quiet times when interruptions aren't welcome, or creating agreements about household responsibilities that work for both brain types.

Communication Adjustments and Couple's Exercises

AuDHD brains process information differently, which means communication strategies that work for neurotypical couples might miss the mark entirely. Adjusting your communication style isn't about walking on eggshells - it's about speaking each other's language more fluently.

Direct communication often works better than hints or subtle suggestions. AuDHD individuals frequently struggle with inference and may miss implied meanings. Instead of "The kitchen's a mess," try "Would you be able to load the dishwasher before dinner?" This clarity prevents confusion and eliminates the guesswork that can lead to misunderstandings.

Processing time becomes a relationship tool rather than an obstacle. When discussing important topics, build in pauses for information processing. You might say, "I'd like to talk about our vacation plans. Would you like to discuss it now, or would you prefer time to think about it first?" This approach respects different cognitive speeds without creating pressure.

Written communication can supplement verbal discussions, especially for complex topics. Some couples find that sharing thoughts via email or text before in-person conversations helps the AuDHD partner organize their thoughts and reduces anxiety about forgetting important points during discussion.

Sensory considerations during serious conversations matter more than many couples realize. Choosing quiet environments, avoiding conversations when your partner is overstimulated, and being mindful of physical comfort can dramatically improve communication effectiveness.

Validation techniques require calibration for AuDHD experiences. Instead of minimizing concerns ("It's not that bad"), acknowledge the reality of their experience ("That sounds really overwhelming"). Validation doesn't mean agreement - it means recognizing that their perception is real and deserves respect.

Exercise 1: The Daily Check-In

Establish a brief daily routine where you each share:

- Energy level (1-10)
- Any sensory challenges anticipated or experienced
- One thing you need from each other
- One appreciation

This five-minute conversation prevents small issues from building into large conflicts and keeps you connected to each other's internal experiences.

Exercise 2: The Communication Preference Map

Together, identify your individual preferences for:

- Best times of day for important conversations

- Preferred environments for different types of discussions
- Processing time needed for various topics
- Warning signs that someone needs a communication break

Create a visual map you can both reference when planning discussions.

Exercise 3: The Conflict Resolution Ritual

Develop a structured approach for addressing disagreements:

1. **Pause**: Either person can call for a break if emotions are too high
2. **Perspective**: Each person shares their viewpoint without interruption
3. **Clarify**: Ask questions to ensure understanding
4. **Collaborate**: Work together on solutions that honor both perspectives
5. **Check**: Follow up later to ensure the solution is working

Exercise 4: The Appreciation Practice

Weekly, share:

- One way your partner's AuDHD traits brought something positive to your week
- One accommodation or adjustment that made a difference
- One thing you're learning about yourself through this process

This practice rewires your brain to notice strengths rather than focusing only on challenges.

Exercise 5: The Energy Management Plan

Map out your weekly schedules together, identifying:

- High-demand activities that require recovery time

- Low-energy options for difficult days
- Sensory-friendly alternatives for social obligations
- Backup plans for when original plans become overwhelming

This collaborative approach prevents energy depletion and reduces conflict around social commitments.

Nonverbal communication adjustments can be particularly important. AuDHD individuals may have difficulty reading facial expressions, body language, or tone of voice. Being more explicit about your emotional state ("I'm feeling frustrated, but not with you") prevents misinterpretation and reduces anxiety.

Timing conversations strategically improves outcomes significantly. Avoid important discussions when your partner is overstimulated, tired, or transitioning between activities. Many AuDHD individuals have specific times of day when their cognitive resources are highest - learning these patterns helps you communicate more effectively.

Conflict resolution requires patience and structure. During disagreements, focus on specific behaviors rather than character judgments. Instead of "You're being difficult," try "When plans change suddenly, it seems to stress you out. How can we handle changes in a way that works better for both of us?"

The goal isn't to eliminate all challenges from your relationship - it's to understand them well enough that you can navigate them together. Every couple faces obstacles; yours just happen to involve sensory processing differences, executive function variations, and social energy management. With understanding and adjustment, these differences become part of your unique partnership rather than sources of ongoing conflict.

Chapter 13: Family Support Strategies

Being the Support System, They Need

Supporting a family member through AuDHD discovery requires a fundamental shift in perspective. This isn't about fixing someone or helping them become more "normal" - it's about understanding how their brain works and creating an environment where they can thrive authentically. Family support during this period can make the difference between shame-filled struggle and empowered self-acceptance.

The discovery process affects the entire family system, not just the diagnosed individual. Siblings may feel confused about changes in family dynamics. Parents might experience guilt about missed signs or past misunderstandings. Extended family members could struggle with acceptance or understanding. Recognizing that this is a family journey, not just an individual one, helps everyone adjust more successfully.

Many families initially focus on what needs to change about their AuDHD member, but the most supportive families ask what needs to change about their systems, expectations, and approaches. This perspective shift transforms diagnosis from a problem to be solved into an opportunity for deeper understanding and stronger connections.

Understanding the Grief Process and Providing Practical Support

The grief process for AuDHD discovery is complex and often misunderstood by well-meaning family members. Unlike grief from loss, this grief involves mourning while simultaneously celebrating. Your family member is grieving missed opportunities, misunderstood experiences, and years of unnecessary struggle, while also celebrating finally having answers and a path forward.

The stages of AuDHD grief don't follow a linear pattern. Your family member might cycle through anger at missed diagnosis, sadness about past struggles, relief about having answers, and fear about the future - sometimes all in the same day. Understanding this emotional complexity helps you respond with appropriate support rather than trying to "fix" their feelings.

Anger often emerges toward family members, medical professionals, teachers, or themselves. This anger isn't personal, even when it feels directed at you. It's processing decades of being misunderstood, criticized for traits they couldn't control, or forced to mask their authentic selves. Responding with defensiveness only escalates conflict. Instead, acknowledge their experience: "It makes sense that you're angry about not getting support earlier."

Sadness frequently focuses on lost opportunities - the friendships that might have been possible with better understanding, the academic or career paths that could have been pursued with appropriate support, the years spent believing something was fundamentally wrong with them. This sadness is productive and necessary for healing. Resist the urge to minimize it with statements like "But look how successful you are now."

Relief and validation often alternate with grief. Your family member might express joy about finally understanding themselves, followed by sadness about how long it took. Both emotions are valid and necessary. Celebrate the understanding while holding space for the grief.

Fear about the future commonly emerges as they process what AuDHD means for their relationships, career, and life plans. They might worry about discrimination, whether people will treat them differently, or if they'll be able to maintain their current lifestyle. These fears deserve acknowledgment and practical problem-solving support rather than dismissal.

Practical support during this period focuses on reducing barriers and increasing accessibility. This might involve:

Research assistance: Help them find neurodivergent-affirming therapists, support groups, or educational resources. Many newly diagnosed individuals feel overwhelmed by the amount of information available and appreciate help organizing and prioritizing resources.

Accommodation planning: Support them in identifying what changes might help at home, work, or in social situations. This could involve rearranging living spaces to reduce sensory overwhelm, helping them practice disclosure conversations, or brainstorming solutions for executive function challenges.

Emotional regulation support: Learn to recognize when they're approaching overwhelm and offer practical assistance. This might mean taking over tasks temporarily, providing sensory tools, or simply giving them space to decompress without taking their need for solitude personally.

Advocacy assistance: Help them navigate systems that might not understand neurodivergent needs. This could involve attending medical appointments, helping draft accommodation requests, or providing moral support during difficult conversations.

Self-Care for Family Members and Celebrating Neurodiversity

Supporting someone through AuDHD discovery while maintaining your own well-being requires intentional self-care strategies. Family members often become so focused on providing support that they neglect their own needs, leading to burnout, resentment, and reduced effectiveness as supporters.

Emotional self-care involves processing your own feelings about the diagnosis separately from supporting your family member. You might experience relief at finally understanding confusing behaviors, guilt about past interactions, worry about the future, or grief about your own assumptions being challenged. These feelings deserve attention and care.

Consider joining support groups for families of neurodivergent individuals, working with a therapist who understands neurodivergent family dynamics, or connecting with other families navigating similar experiences. Online communities can provide valuable perspective and practical advice from people who understand your situation.

Physical self-care becomes especially important when supporting someone through an intensive adjustment period. The stress of learning new information, adjusting family systems, and providing emotional support can be physically exhausting. Maintain your exercise routines, sleep schedule, and nutrition habits even when family life feels chaotic.

Social self-care means maintaining relationships and activities outside of your family's adjustment process. Continue spending time with friends, pursuing hobbies, and engaging in activities that bring you joy. This isn't selfish - it's essential for maintaining the emotional resources needed to be supportive long-term.

Intellectual self-care involves learning about AuDHD from multiple sources rather than relying solely on your family member to educate you. Read books, attend webinars, or take courses about neurodivergent experiences. This knowledge helps you provide better support while reducing the educational burden on your family member.

Setting boundaries protects both your well-being and your ability to provide sustainable support. This might involve agreeing on specific times for AuDHD-related discussions, establishing limits on research or planning assistance you can provide, or maintaining your own commitments and responsibilities despite family changes.

Celebrating neurodiversity within your family creates an atmosphere of acceptance rather than deficit-focused thinking. This involves recognizing and appreciating the unique strengths your AuDHD family member brings to your family system.

AuDHD individuals often contribute:

- *Intense passion and expertise* in their areas of interest

- *Honest and direct communication* that reduces family guesswork
- *Creative problem-solving approaches* to household or personal challenges
- *Deep empathy* for others who feel different or marginalized
- *Attention to detail* that benefits family planning and decision-making
- *Authentic living* that inspires other family members to be more genuine

Reframing challenges as differences rather than deficits helps the entire family adjust their perspective. Instead of seeing sensory sensitivities as problems, recognize them as detailed environmental awareness. Rather than viewing routine needs as rigidity, appreciate them as stability preferences that can benefit the whole family.

Creating neurodivergent-friendly family traditions demonstrates acceptance and celebration. This might involve establishing sensory-friendly holiday celebrations, incorporating special interests into family activities, or developing communication rituals that work for different brain types.

Educating extended family and friends protects your immediate family from having to constantly explain or defend neurodivergent needs. Take on the role of educating grandparents, aunts, uncles, and family friends about AuDHD so your diagnosed family member doesn't bear the full burden of advocacy.

Family Meeting Templates and Resource Sharing Guides

Structured family meetings provide a safe space for discussing AuDHD-related topics, planning accommodations, and addressing concerns. Regular meetings prevent issues from building up and ensure everyone's voice is heard in family decisions.

Family Meeting Template 1: Initial Diagnosis Discussion

Opening (5 minutes)

- Everyone shares one word describing how they're feeling today
- Review the purpose: understanding and supporting each other

Education Sharing (15 minutes)

- AuDHD family member shares what they've learned about themselves
- Family members ask clarifying questions
- Discuss what this means for understanding past experiences

Impact Discussion (15 minutes)

- How might this change family routines or expectations?
- What accommodations might be helpful at home?
- What concerns or worries does anyone have?

Planning (10 minutes)

- Identify 2-3 immediate changes to try
- Assign any research or preparation tasks
- Schedule follow-up conversation

Closing (5 minutes)

- Each person shares one thing they learned
- Plan something enjoyable to do together

Family Meeting Template 2: Accommodation Planning

Check-in (10 minutes)

- How are current accommodations working?
- Any new challenges or successes to discuss?

Specific Planning (20 minutes)

- Focus on one area (home environment, social situations, communication, etc.)
- Brainstorm solutions together
- Consider impact on all family members

Resource Review (10 minutes)

- Share helpful articles, videos, or tools discovered
- Discuss upcoming appointments or events requiring planning
- Review budget considerations for accommodations

Next Steps (10 minutes)

- Assign action items with timelines
- Schedule any necessary conversations with outside parties
- Plan follow-up check-in

Family Meeting Template 3: Extended Family Preparation

Preparation Review (10 minutes)

- Which family events or gatherings are coming up?
- What accommodations or preparations would be helpful?

Education Planning (15 minutes)

- What do extended family members need to understand?
- Who will take responsibility for educating them?
- Practice conversations that might be needed

Support Strategy (15 minutes)

- How will family members support each other during gatherings?
- What signals or code words might be helpful?
- Plan exit strategies if needed

Resource Sharing (10 minutes)

- Share articles or materials appropriate for extended family
- Discuss how to handle inappropriate comments or questions
- Review positive examples to share

Resource Sharing Guide for Families

Educational Resources to Share:

- Age-appropriate books about neurodivergence for children
- Articles explaining AuDHD that avoid overly clinical language
- Videos featuring positive neurodivergent role models
- Information about famous successful people who are AuDHD

Practical Resource Categories:

- *Sensory tools*: websites for fidgets, noise-canceling headphones, weighted blankets
- *Organization systems*: apps, planners, and tools that work with executive function differences
- *Communication aids*: visual schedules, social scripts, and conversation supports
- *Professional services*: directories for neurodivergent-affirming therapists, coaches, and medical providers

Community Resources:

- Local support groups for families and individuals
- Neurodivergent social groups and activity clubs
- Educational workshops and conferences
- Online communities for ongoing support and information sharing

Emergency Resources:

- Crisis hotlines familiar with neurodivergent experiences
- Hospital or medical facilities with neurodivergent-friendly protocols
- Respite care options for family caregiver relief
- Legal resources for discrimination or accommodation issues

Creating a family resource library ensures everyone has access to information and tools. This might be a physical binder, shared digital folder, or family website where everyone can contribute helpful discoveries. Regular resource sharing keeps the family informed and reduces the research burden on any single member.

The goal of family support isn't to eliminate all challenges or make your AuDHD family member more neurotypical. It's to create an environment where they can be authentically themselves while having their needs met and their strengths celebrated. This approach benefits everyone in the family by promoting acceptance, creativity, and genuine connection over conformity and performance.

Building on this foundation of family support and understanding naturally leads us to examine how these principles extend into parenting approaches and breaking generational patterns of misunderstanding, particularly when AuDHD traits appear across generations in your family system.

Chapter 14: Parenting and Generational Patterns

Breaking Cycles, Building Understanding

Discovering your own AuDHD often illuminates patterns that stretch across generations. You might suddenly understand why your child struggles in ways that feel familiar, or recognize traits in your parents that were dismissed as personality quirks decades ago. This recognition brings both relief and responsibility - the relief of understanding family patterns and the responsibility of breaking cycles that may have caused unnecessary pain.

Parenting with AuDHD awareness changes everything. It shifts focus from trying to make children fit neurotypical expectations to helping them understand and work with their unique brains. This approach requires unlearning much of what you may have been taught about "good parenting" and replacing those assumptions with neurodivergent-affirming practices.

The guilt that often accompanies this discovery can feel overwhelming. Many parents find themselves replaying years of interactions, wondering how many meltdowns were actually overwhelm, how many "behavioral problems" were unmet sensory needs, or how many struggles could have been prevented with better understanding. This guilt, while natural, serves no one. What matters now is using your newfound awareness to create positive change for your family.

Recognizing AuDHD in Children and Healing Parenting Guilt

AuDHD in children often presents differently than adult presentations, partly because children are still developing coping mechanisms and haven't learned to mask as extensively. However, masking can begin surprisingly early, especially in children who receive negative feedback about their natural behaviors or who observe that their way of being creates problems for others.

Early signs might include sensory sensitivities that seem extreme to others - covering ears at birthday parties, refusing certain clothing textures, or becoming distressed by changes in routine. These aren't defiance or attention-seeking behaviors; they're neurological responses to overwhelming input or unexpected changes.

Executive function challenges in AuDHD children often manifest as forgetfulness, difficulty with transitions, trouble organizing belongings, or seeming to "tune out" during instructions. Parents frequently interpret these as willful disobedience or lack of caring, leading to power struggles that benefit no one.

Social differences may include preferring adult conversation to peer interaction, intense friendships with one or two people rather than large social groups, or difficulty understanding unwritten social rules. These children might seem mature in some ways while appearing naive in others, creating confusion for both parents and teachers.

Intense interests are common and can be incredibly detailed and focused. A child might know everything about trains, spend hours drawing the same character repeatedly, or become upset when their interests aren't shared or respected by others. These passions are often sources of joy and expertise rather than problems to be redirected.

Emotional regulation differences can be particularly challenging for families. AuDHD children might have intense reactions to seemingly minor events, take a long time to calm down from upset, or struggle to identify and communicate their emotional needs. What looks like "overreacting" is often appropriate responding to experiences that feel genuinely overwhelming.

The masking dilemma presents unique challenges. Children who learn to mask their AuDHD traits may appear to function well in school while falling apart at home, using all their energy to appear "normal" in public settings. This can create confusion for parents who see reports of good behavior from teachers while dealing with meltdowns and exhaustion at home.

Healing parenting guilt requires recognizing that you parented with the information and understanding available to you at the time. Guilt implies you intentionally chose harmful approaches, which isn't accurate. You responded to your child's behaviors with the frameworks you had - frameworks that unfortunately weren't designed with neurodivergent needs in mind.

Reframing past interactions helps process guilt productively. That time you insisted your child "just try" a food that made them gag wasn't cruelty - it was operating from assumptions about typical sensory processing. The consequences you gave for "not listening" when they couldn't process multiple instructions weren't punishment for the sake of meanness - they reflected misunderstanding about how their brain handled information.

Self-forgiveness practice becomes essential for healing. Write letters to yourself acknowledging your good intentions, the love behind your actions, and your commitment to doing better with new understanding. Recognize that discovering your child's neurodivergence doesn't erase years of love, care, and positive parenting - it simply adds new tools to your toolkit.

Making amends with your child can help both of you heal, but approach this carefully based on your child's age and emotional capacity. Young children might benefit from simple acknowledgments: "I'm learning that your brain works differently than I understood before, and I'm going to do better at helping you with things that are hard." Older children might appreciate more detailed conversations about past misunderstandings and your commitment to change.

Focusing on repair rather than regret channels guilt into productive action. Instead of dwelling on past mistakes, concentrate on understanding your child's current needs and creating systems that support their success. Every day offers new opportunities to parent with neurodivergent awareness.

Creating Neurodivergent-Affirming Households

A neurodivergent-affirming household operates on principles of acceptance, accommodation, and celebration rather than normalization and compliance. This doesn't mean chaos or lack of structure - it means structure that serves neurodivergent needs rather than fighting against them.

Environmental modifications create spaces where AuDHD family members can thrive. This might involve creating quiet zones for sensory breaks, establishing visual organization systems that work with executive function differences, or setting up spaces that accommodate special interests and stimming needs.

Lighting considerations matter more than most families realize. Fluorescent lights can be overwhelming for sensory-sensitive individuals, while natural light or warm LED alternatives create calmer environments. Consider dimmer switches, lamps with adjustable brightness, or colored lights that can be modified based on sensory needs.

Sound management helps create sensory-friendly homes. This might involve sound-dampening materials in common areas, designated quiet times when loud activities aren't permitted, or providing noise-canceling headphones for family members who need them during noisy activities.

Organization systems work with AuDHD brains rather than against them. Visual organization - clear containers, labels with pictures, color-coding systems - helps executive function challenges while reducing daily frustration. "A place for everything and everything in its place" becomes especially important when working memory and attention differences make finding misplaced items particularly difficult.

Sensory accommodations throughout the home normalize different sensory needs. This might include weighted blankets available in common areas, fidget toys in designated containers, different seating options (wobble cushions, bean bags, firm chairs), or sensory-friendly clothing options readily accessible.

Routine flexibility balances the need for predictable structure with accommodation for AuDHD variability. Establish core routines that provide security while building in flexibility for days when sensory needs, energy levels, or executive function capacity differ from typical.

Morning routines might include visual schedules that can be adjusted based on daily needs, buffer time for processing and transitions, and sensory preparation activities that help regulate nervous systems for the day ahead.

Evening routines often need to account for sensory overwhelm accumulated throughout the day, providing opportunities for decompression, special interest time, and calming activities that help transition to rest.

Weekly rhythms can accommodate energy patterns and processing needs. Some families find that scheduling demanding activities on certain days while keeping others lighter works better than trying to maintain identical daily schedules.

Communication adaptations ensure all family members can express their needs and be understood. This involves learning each person's communication style and adjusting family communication patterns accordingly.

Direct communication often works better than hints or implications. "Please put your dishes in the dishwasher after eating" is clearer than "The kitchen's getting messy." This directness isn't rude - it's accessible.

Processing time becomes a family value. Before expecting immediate responses to questions or requests, allow thinking time. "I need to think about that" becomes an acceptable response that's respected rather than pressured.

Visual communication supports help with executive function and processing differences. Family calendars, chore charts with pictures, and written reminders supplement verbal communication and reduce memory demands.

Emotional check-ins help family members identify and communicate their internal states. Simple systems like numbered energy levels, color-coded mood indicators, or agreed-upon signals for needing space create communication pathways for experiences that might be hard to articulate.

Celebrating neurodivergence means recognizing and valuing the unique contributions each family member brings. AuDHD individuals often contribute creativity, intense expertise, honest feedback, attention to detail, and passionate engagement that enriches family life.

Special interests become family learning opportunities rather than sources of annoyance. When one family member becomes passionate about astronomy, the whole family might visit planetariums, read space books together, or incorporate constellation viewing into family activities.

Different abilities are appreciated rather than seen as deficits. The family member who notices details others miss becomes the family's quality control specialist. The one who hyperfocuses becomes the go-to person for research projects. The one who thinks differently becomes the creative problem-solver.

Advocacy skills develop naturally in neurodivergent-affirming families. Children learn to identify their needs, ask for accommodations, and explain their experiences to others. Parents model respectful advocacy and teach children how to stand up for themselves and others.

School Advocacy and Family Neurodiversity Mapping

School advocacy for AuDHD children requires understanding both your child's specific needs and the educational system's capabilities and limitations. Effective advocacy balances pushing for appropriate accommodations with building collaborative relationships with school staff.

Understanding your rights provides the foundation for effective advocacy. AuDHD children may qualify for accommodations under Section 504 plans or services under Individualized Education Programs (IEPs), depending on how their differences impact their educational access.

504 Plans provide accommodations that help level the playing field without changing academic expectations. These might include extended time on tests, breaks during long activities, preferential seating, or modified homework expectations.

IEP services provide specialized instruction and support for children whose disabilities significantly impact their educational progress. AuDHD children might receive occupational therapy for sensory needs, speech therapy for social communication, or specialized instruction for executive function skills.

Informal accommodations often provide the most immediate relief while formal processes unfold. Working with individual teachers to implement sensory breaks, modified assignments, or communication adjustments can improve your child's school experience significantly.

Preparing for school meetings increases your effectiveness as an advocate. Document your child's needs with specific examples, research potential accommodations, and prepare talking points that focus on helping your child access education rather than creating extra work for teachers.

Data collection strengthens your advocacy. Keep records of meltdowns, school avoidance, homework struggles, or social difficulties that correlate with school demands. This information helps school staff understand the impact of current approaches and the need for modifications.

Strength identification helps reframe conversations from deficit-focused to strength-based. Prepare examples of your child's capabilities, interests, and positive contributions to share alongside areas of difficulty.

Accommodation research allows you to suggest specific solutions rather than just identifying problems. Learn about accommodations that have worked for other AuDHD children and come prepared with concrete suggestions.

Building collaborative relationships with school staff creates better outcomes than adversarial approaches. Most educators want to help children succeed but may lack understanding about neurodivergent needs.

Education approaches work better than demanding compliance. Share resources about AuDHD, explain how your child's brain works differently, and help staff understand the "why" behind behavioral differences.

Solution-focused meetings emphasize problem-solving together rather than placing blame. Frame discussions around "How can we help this child succeed?" rather than "What's wrong with current approaches?"

Regular communication prevents small issues from becoming large conflicts. Establish systems for ongoing communication between home and school that allow for quick adjustments and collaborative problem-solving.

Family neurodiversity mapping helps you understand patterns across generations and identify both strengths and support needs within your family system. This process can reveal why certain approaches work well for your family while others create consistent conflict.

Family Neurodiversity Mapping Exercise

Step 1: Individual Assessment For each family member, identify:

- Sensory preferences and sensitivities
- Communication styles and needs

- Energy patterns and optimal performance times
- Special interests and areas of expertise
- Executive function strengths and challenges
- Social preferences and needs

Step 2: Pattern Recognition Look for patterns across generations:

- Which traits appear in multiple family members?
- What strategies have worked well for different individuals?
- Where do conflicts typically arise between different neurocognitive styles?
- What family strengths emerge from neurodivergent traits?

Step 3: System Analysis Examine how family systems support or challenge different neurotypes:

- Which family routines work well for everyone?
- Where do accommodations for one person create challenges for others?
- How can family systems be modified to support all members?
- What external support would benefit the family system?

Step 4: Strength Integration Identify how different neurotypes contribute to family success:

- Who serves as the family's attention to detail specialist?
- Who brings creative problem-solving to family challenges?
- Who provides emotional sensitivity and empathy?
- Who contributes organization and planning skills?

Step 5: Support Planning Develop family support strategies that honor different needs:

- How can family members support each other during difficult times?
- What accommodations would benefit multiple family members?
- How can conflicts between different neurotypes be resolved respectfully?
- What professional support would benefit the family system?

This mapping process helps families understand that neurodivergence isn't a problem to be solved but a set of differences to be understood and accommodated. It reveals how diversity strengthens families and provides frameworks for supporting all members effectively.

Intergenerational healing often emerges from this understanding. Parents might recognize their own childhood struggles in their children's experiences, leading to healing conversations with their own parents or renewed commitment to breaking cycles of misunderstanding.

Grandparent education becomes an opportunity for family healing. Sharing neurodivergent understanding with older generations can help them reframe their own parenting experiences and develop better relationships with neurodivergent grandchildren.

Sibling support ensures that neurotypical children understand and support their neurodivergent siblings while having their own needs respected and met. This might involve explaining why different children need different approaches and teaching advocacy skills.

Extended family preparation helps create supportive environments during family gatherings. Sharing information about sensory needs, communication styles, and behavioral differences prevents misunderstandings and creates more inclusive family experiences.

The goal of neurodivergent-affirming parenting isn't to eliminate all challenges or make children indistinguishable from their neurotypical peers. It's to help children understand their own brains, develop effective strategies, and build confidence in their unique ways of experiencing the world. This foundation enables them to advocate for themselves and thrive authentically throughout their lives.

This understanding of generational patterns and family systems naturally guides us toward considering how to design sustainable, authentic lives that honor neurodivergent needs while building meaningful connections and contributions to broader communities.

Chapter 15: Your Authentic Future

Designing a Life That Fits

Living authentically with AuDHD isn't about finding a perfect life where challenges disappear - it's about creating a life that works with your brain rather than against it. This means designing systems, relationships, and goals that honor your sensory needs, executive function patterns, energy cycles, and authentic interests rather than forcing yourself into neurotypical templates that drain your resources and diminish your well-being.

The process of designing an authentic future begins with releasing the life you thought you should want and embracing the life that actually fits. This can feel scary because it means letting go of external expectations and trusting your internal compass. Yet this trust becomes the foundation for building a sustainable, fulfilling life that leverages your unique strengths while accommodating your specific challenges.

Your authentic future isn't something you discover once and implement permanently. It's an ongoing practice of checking in with yourself, adjusting when something isn't working, and having the courage to make changes that support your well-being even when others don't understand your choices.

Long-Term Planning and Aging Considerations

Traditional life planning often assumes linear career progression, standard relationship timelines, and predictable aging patterns. AuDHD individuals frequently need different approaches that account for energy variability, sensory changes, executive function evolution, and the cumulative effects of masking or accommodating neurotypical expectations.

Career planning with AuDHD requires thinking beyond traditional employment structures. While some individuals thrive in conventional careers with appropriate accommodations, others find fulfillment in entrepreneurship, freelancing, or non-traditional work arrangements that offer greater flexibility and alignment with their natural rhythms.

Energy management becomes central to career sustainability. Consider how different work environments, schedules, and demands affect your long-term capacity. A high-paying job that requires constant masking might be less sustainable than a lower-paying position that allows authentic functioning.

Skills development can focus on leveraging natural interests and abilities rather than forcing growth in areas that consistently drain your resources. This doesn't mean avoiding all challenging areas, but rather building careers around strengths while developing workarounds for difficulties.

Accommodation planning involves anticipating needs that might change over time. Sensory sensitivities might increase with age, executive function demands might become more challenging, or social energy might decrease. Building flexibility into career plans allows for adjustments without deriving your sense of success.

Relationship planning acknowledges that AuDHD individuals may have different relationship needs and timelines than neurotypical expectations suggest. Some people thrive in traditional relationship structures while others need modified approaches to intimacy, commitment, and shared living.

Social energy budgeting becomes a lifelong practice. Plan relationships and social obligations around your actual capacity rather than attempting to meet external expectations that leave you consistently depleted.

Communication evolution continues throughout life as you develop better understanding of your needs and more effective ways of expressing them. Early relationships might involve significant masking, while later relationships can benefit from your increased self-awareness and advocacy skills.

Support system planning involves cultivating relationships that provide genuine support rather than just social compliance. This might mean smaller social circles with deeper connections, relationships based on shared interests rather than convenience, or friendships that accommodate your communication style and energy patterns.

Financial planning requires accounting for AuDHD-specific costs and earning patterns. You might need to budget for sensory accommodations, therapeutic support, organization systems, or periods of reduced earning capacity due to burnout or health challenges.

Accommodation costs can be significant over time. Noise-canceling headphones, ergonomic furniture, specialized clothing, dietary needs, or modified living spaces represent investments in your well-being rather than optional expenses.

Healthcare planning becomes especially important as understanding of adult AuDHD evolves. Budget for ongoing therapeutic support, medication costs, and healthcare providers who understand neurodivergent needs.

Career flexibility funds provide security for periods when traditional employment might not be sustainable. Having financial cushions for career transitions, health challenges, or burnout recovery protects your long-term well-being.

Aging considerations acknowledge that AuDHD traits may evolve over time, sometimes in unexpected ways. What works in your twenties and thirties might need adjustment as your brain and body change.

Sensory changes can occur with normal aging, potentially intensifying existing sensitivities or creating new ones. Plan living environments and daily routines with flexibility for evolving sensory needs.

Executive function evolution might mean that systems that once worked become inadequate, requiring ongoing adjustment and support. This isn't failure - it's normal adaptation to changing capacities.

Social energy patterns often shift with age, sometimes leading to decreased tolerance for large social gatherings or increased preference for meaningful one-on-one connections. Plan social lives that can adapt to these changes.

Health advocacy needs increase with age as medical systems often lack understanding of how aging intersects with neurodivergence. Build relationships with healthcare providers who respect your self-knowledge and accommodate your communication needs.

Building Sustainable Support Systems and Community Contribution

Sustainable support systems for AuDHD individuals require intentional cultivation of relationships and resources that provide genuine assistance without creating overwhelming social obligations. This balance between receiving support and maintaining autonomy is crucial for long-term well-being.

Professional support teams might include various specialists who understand neurodivergent needs. This isn't about having problems that need fixing - it's about having resources available for different life challenges and transitions.

Therapeutic support can provide ongoing assistance with emotional regulation, relationship challenges, life transitions, or trauma processing. Look for therapists who understand neurodivergence as difference rather than disorder.

Medical advocacy becomes essential as you age and encounter healthcare providers who may not understand AuDHD presentations or dismiss self-reported symptoms. Consider having advocates who can accompany you to appointments or help communicate your needs.

Executive function support might involve professional organizers, virtual assistants, or coaches who help with planning, time management, or project completion. These services can prevent burnout and increase your capacity for activities you find meaningful.

Career support could include mentors in your field, career coaches who understand neurodivergent workplace needs, or professional networks that provide both opportunities and advocacy.

Peer support networks offer connection with others who share similar experiences and can provide both practical advice and emotional understanding. These relationships often feel more natural and less draining than traditional social connections.

Online communities provide access to support regardless of geographic location and allow for participation based on your energy and availability. Many AuDHD individuals find online connections easier to maintain than in-person relationships.

Local support groups offer face-to-face connection and practical resource sharing. These groups might focus on specific aspects of AuDHD experience, life stages, or shared interests.

Mentorship relationships can develop naturally within neurodivergent communities, offering opportunities to both receive and provide guidance based on lived experience.

Community contribution allows you to share your unique perspectives and abilities while building meaningful connections. Contributing to communities doesn't require traditional volunteer models that might not fit your needs or capacity.

Interest-based contribution leverages your special interests and expertise. This might involve sharing knowledge through writing, teaching, or consulting in areas where you have deep knowledge and passion.

Advocacy activities can range from informal education within your circles to more formal activism, depending on your capacity and interests. Your lived experience provides valuable perspective for improving understanding and systems.

Skill sharing within neurodivergent communities helps others while utilizing your strengths. This might involve teaching coping strategies, sharing accommodation successes, or providing peer support.

Creative expression can contribute to cultural understanding of neurodivergence while providing personal fulfillment. This might involve art, writing, performance, or other creative outlets that share your perspective.

Reciprocal relationships create balanced exchanges that prevent the exhaustion that can come from one-sided giving or receiving. Look for relationships where your contributions are valued and your needs are respected.

Skill exchanges with other neurodivergent individuals can provide mutual support. You might help someone with organization while they assist you with social navigation, creating beneficial partnerships.

Interest communities built around shared passions often provide natural reciprocity. Contributing your expertise while learning from others creates satisfying exchange relationships.

Advocacy partnerships allow you to support causes you care about while working alongside others who share your values and understand your communication style.

Personal Manifesto Creation and Life Design Workshop

Creating a personal manifesto helps clarify your values, priorities, and commitments in language that resonates with your authentic self. This document serves as a compass for decision-making and a reminder of what matters most when external pressures try to pull you away from your chosen path.

Values clarification forms the foundation of your manifesto. AuDHD individuals often have strong values around authenticity, justice, competence, and meaningful work, but may have learned to suppress these values in favor of social acceptability.

Core values identification involves reflecting on what matters most to you regardless of others' expectations. Consider moments when you felt most aligned with yourself and identify the values that were being honored in those experiences.

Values prioritization helps when different values conflict. You might value both community connection and solitude - understanding which takes priority in different circumstances helps guide decisions.

Values application translates abstract concepts into concrete choices. If authenticity is a core value, what does that mean for career choices, relationships, and daily decisions?

Life principles development creates guidelines for navigating challenges and decisions. These principles reflect your understanding of how to live well with your particular brain and circumstances.

Energy management principles might include commitments to honoring your natural rhythms, building recovery time into busy periods, and saying no to activities that consistently drain more than they contribute.

Relationship principles could involve commitments to direct communication, mutual respect for different neurotypes, and maintaining connections that support your authentic self.

Growth principles might emphasize learning through interests rather than external requirements, accepting your current capacity while working toward sustainable expansion, and celebrating progress rather than demanding perfection.

Contribution principles could focus on sharing your gifts in ways that align with your values and capacity rather than meeting others' expectations of how you should contribute.

Personal Manifesto Template

My Core Values List 3-5 values that are most important to you, with brief descriptions of what each means in your life.

My Life Principles Describe the guidelines you want to follow in major life areas:

- Energy and self-care
- Relationships and communication
- Work and contribution
- Growth and learning
- Decision-making and priorities

My Commitments State specific commitments you're making to yourself:

- What will you do to honor your needs?
- How will you handle conflicts between your needs and others' expectations?
- What boundaries will you maintain?
- How will you measure success and well-being?

My Vision Describe the life you want to create:

- What does an authentic life look like for you?
- How do you want to contribute to your communities?
- What legacy do you want to leave?
- What would make you proud of the life you've built?

Life Design Workshop provides structured opportunities to translate your manifesto into actionable plans. This isn't about creating rigid goals but rather about designing flexible frameworks that support your authentic living.

Workshop Exercise 1: Life Area Assessment

Rate your current satisfaction (1-10) in each area and identify what would need to change to increase satisfaction:

- **Work/Career**: Does your work align with your values and accommodate your needs?
- **Relationships**: Do your relationships support your authentic self?
- **Living Environment**: Does your home environment support your sensory and organizational needs?
- **Health and Well-being**: Are you managing your physical and mental health effectively?
- **Community and Contribution**: Are you connected to communities where you can both give and receive?
- **Personal Growth**: Are you learning and developing in ways that interest you?
- **Recreation and Interests**: Do you have time and space for activities that bring you joy?

Workshop Exercise 2: Obstacle and Resource Mapping

For areas where you want to create change:

Identify obstacles: What internal or external barriers make change difficult?

- Executive function challenges
- Financial constraints
- Social expectations
- Fear or anxiety
- Lack of information or support

Map resources: What assets do you have available?

- Personal strengths and skills
- Supportive relationships
- Financial resources
- Professional support
- Community connections
- Knowledge and experience

Workshop Exercise 3: Sustainable Change Planning

Choose 1-2 areas for focused attention and create realistic change plans:

Small steps identification: What tiny changes could you make immediately? **System building**: What routines or structures would support ongoing change? **Support activation**: Who or what could help you maintain momentum? **Progress tracking**: How will you know if changes are working? **Flexibility planning**: How will you adjust if original plans don't work?

Workshop Exercise 4: Authenticity Check

For each area of your life, ask:

- Am I doing this because I want to or because I think I should?
- Does this activity/relationship/commitment energize or drain me?
- If I could design this area perfectly for my brain, what would it look like?
- What would I need to change to feel more authentic in this area?

The goal of life design isn't to create a perfect plan but to develop ongoing practices of self-reflection, values-based decision-making, and authentic living. Your manifesto and design frameworks will evolve as you grow and change, serving as tools for navigating life with intention rather than rigid blueprints for predetermined outcomes.

Implementation strategies focus on sustainable change rather than dramatic transformation. Small, consistent adjustments often create more lasting change than major overhauls that overwhelm your system.

Gradual implementation allows your nervous system to adjust to changes without triggering overwhelm or resistance. Make one small change at a time and let it integrate before adding new elements.

Regular review keeps your plans relevant and useful. Schedule periodic check-ins with yourself to assess what's working, what needs adjustment, and what new insights you've gained.

Flexibility maintenance allows your plans to evolve with your understanding and circumstances. Rigid adherence to original plans can become just another source of pressure rather than support for authentic living.

The authentic future you're designing isn't a destination you'll reach but a way of living you'll continually refine. Each day offers opportunities to choose authenticity over conformity, self-compassion over self-criticism, and values-based decisions over fear-based reactions. This ongoing practice of authentic living becomes your contribution to a world that desperately needs the perspectives, creativity, and wisdom that come from minds that see and experience life differently.

Moving Into Possibility

Your journey with AuDHD discovery has brought you to this point of possibility - a place where understanding meets action, where self-knowledge transforms into authentic living, and where the challenges you've faced become sources of wisdom and strength. The frameworks, tools, and insights you've explored throughout this guide provide foundations for building a life that truly fits your unique brain and authentic self.

This isn't the end of your discovery but the beginning of intentional living with AuDHD awareness. Every day brings new opportunities to apply what you've learned, to advocate for your needs, to build supportive relationships, and to contribute your unique gifts to communities that benefit from your perspective. Your authentic future awaits your courageous embrace of who you truly are.

References

ACAS. (2023). *Reasonable adjustments for mental health, autism and ADHD at work.* Advisory, Conciliation and Arbitration Service. https://www.acas.org.uk/reasonable-adjustments

American Psychiatric Association. (2022). *Diagnostic and Statistical Manual of Mental Disorders* (5th ed., text rev.). American Psychiatric Publishing.

Antshel, K. M., Zhang-James, Y., Wagner, K., Ledesma, A., & Faraone, S. V. (2016). An update on the comorbidity of ASD and ADHD: A focus on clinical management. *Expert Review of Neurotherapeutics, 16*(3), 279–293. https://doi.org/10.1586/14737175.2016.1146591

Arnold, S. R. C., et al. (2023). Towards the measurement of autistic burnout. *Autism, 27*(5), 1196–1209. https://doi.org/10.1177/13623613221124616

Bargiela, S., Steward, R., & Mandy, W. (2016). The experiences of late-diagnosed women with autism spectrum conditions: An investigation of the female autism phenotype. *Journal of Autism and Developmental Disorders, 46*(10), 3281–3294. https://doi.org/10.1007/s10803-016-2872-8

Bijlenga, D., et al. (2019). The role of the circadian system in the etiology and pathophysiology of ADHD. *Neuroscience & Biobehavioral Reviews, 96*, 371–378. https://doi.org/10.1016/j.neubiorev.2018.11.012

Conner, C. M., et al. (2023). Suicide risk in autistic people: A review. *Current Developmental Disorders Reports, 10*(3), 225–235. https://doi.org/10.1007/s40474-023-00278-4

Demetriou, E. A., et al. (2019). Executive function in autism spectrum disorder: A review of the literature. *Frontiers in Psychiatry, 10*, 753. https://doi.org/10.3389/fpsyt.2019.00753

DIVA Foundation. (2019). *DIVA-5: Diagnostic Interview for ADHD in Adults (5th ed.).* http://www.divacenter.eu

Equality and Human Rights Commission. (2011). *Employment: Statutory Code of Practice.* Equality Act 2010. https://www.equalityhumanrights.com

Evans, D. W., et al. (2024). Autistic masking and its relationship to mental health and social anxiety. *International Journal of Environmental Research and Public Health, 21*(4), 482. https://doi.org/10.3390/ijerph21040482

GOV.UK. (2025). *Reasonable adjustments at work.* UK Government. https://www.gov.uk/reasonable-adjustments

Higgins, J., et al. (2023). Confirming the nature of autistic burnout. *Autism, 27*(6), 1234–1247. https://doi.org/10.1177/13623613231103782

Hours, A. Z. C., et al. (2022). ASD and ADHD comorbidity: What are we talking about? *Frontiers in Psychiatry, 13*, 887871. https://doi.org/10.3389/fpsyt.2022.887871

Hull, L., Mandy, W., & Petrides, K. V. (2019). Development and validation of the Camouflaging Autistic Traits Questionnaire (CAT-Q). *Autism Research, 12*(10), 1663–1676. https://doi.org/10.1002/aur.2227

Hull, L., et al. (2017). "Putting on my best normal": Social camouflaging in adults with autism spectrum conditions. *Journal of Autism and Developmental Disorders, 47*(8), 2519–2534. https://doi.org/10.1007/s10803-017-3166-5

Kooij, J. J. S., et al. (2019). *DIVA-5: Diagnostic Interview for ADHD in Adults (5th ed.).* DIVA Foundation.

Livingston, L. A., & Happé, F. (2017). Conceptualising compensation in neurodevelopmental disorders. *Journal of Child Psychology and Psychiatry, 58*(9), 936–944. https://doi.org/10.1111/jcpp.12737

National Institute for Health and Care Excellence (NICE). (2012, amended 2021). *Autism spectrum disorder in adults: Diagnosis and management (CG142).* NICE. https://www.nice.org.uk/guidance/cg142

National Institute for Health and Care Excellence (NICE). (2018, last reviewed 2025). *Attention deficit hyperactivity disorder: Diagnosis and management (NG87).* NICE. https://www.nice.org.uk/guidance/ng87

NICE. (2018). *Autism-Spectrum Quotient-10 (AQ-10) for adults.* https://www.nice.org.uk/guidance/cg142/resources

Nogueira, H. A., et al. (2023). Melatonin for sleep disorders in people with autism: Systematic review and meta-analysis. *Journal of Pineal Research, 75*(1), e12859. https://doi.org/10.1111/jpi.12859

Pehlivanidis, A., et al. (2020). Trait-based dimensions discriminating adults with ADHD, ASD, and ADHD/ASD. *Psychiatry Investigation, 17*(1), 29–40. https://doi.org/10.30773/pi.2019.0129

Raymaker, D. M., et al. (2020). "Having all of your internal resources exhausted beyond measure...": Defining autistic burnout. *Autism in Adulthood, 2*(2), 132–143. https://doi.org/10.1089/aut.2019.0079

Robertson, C. E., & Baron-Cohen, S. (2017). Sensory perception in autism. *Nature Reviews Neuroscience, 18*(11), 671–684. https://doi.org/10.1038/nrn.2017.112

Rong, Y., et al. (2021). Prevalence of ADHD in individuals with autism spectrum disorder: A meta-analysis. *The Lancet Psychiatry, 8*(11), 944–955. https://doi.org/10.1016/S2215-0366(21)00274-0

Surman, C. B. H., et al. (2021). Managing sleep in adults with ADHD. *Current Psychiatry Reports, 23*(11), 75. https://doi.org/10.1007/s11920-021-01284-w

Tavassoli, T., et al. (2014). Sensory over-responsivity in adults with autism spectrum conditions. *Autism, 18*(4), 428–432. https://doi.org/10.1177/1362361313477246

UK Government. (2024). *Equality Act 2010: Guidance.* https://www.gov.uk/equality-act-2010-guidance

Willcutt, E. G., Doyle, A. E., Nigg, J. T., Faraone, S. V., & Pennington, B. F. (2005). Validity of the executive function theory of ADHD: A meta-analytic review. *Biological Psychiatry, 57*(11), 1336–1346. https://doi.org/10.1016/j.biopsych.2005.02.006

World Health Organization. (2019/2023). *ICD-11 Clinical descriptions and diagnostic requirements: 6A02 Autism spectrum disorder.* WHO.

World Health Organization. (2019/2023). *ICD-11 Clinical descriptions and diagnostic requirements: 6A05 Attention-deficit/hyperactivity disorder.* WHO.

www.ingramcontent.com/pod-product-compliance
Lightning Source LLC
Chambersburg PA
CBHW062153080426
42734CB00010B/1670